Hustle your way to Property Success

First published in 2011 by Ecademy Press

48 St Vincent Drive, St Albans, Hertfordshire, AL1 5SJ

info@ecademy-press.com www.ecademy-press.com

Printed and Bound by Lightning Source in the UK and USA

Set by Neil Coe

Printed on acid-free paper from managed forests. This book is printed on demand, so no copies will be remaindered or pulped.

ISBN 978-1-907722-57-8

The right of Paul Ribbons to be identified as the author of this work has been asserted in accordance with sections 77 and 78 of the Copyright Designs and Patents Act 1988.

A CIP catalogue record for this book is available from the British Library.

The purpose of this book is to educate and entertain. The author and Ecademy Press shall have neither liability nor responsibility to any person or entity with respect to any loss or damage caused, or alleged to have been caused, directly or indirectly, by the information contained in this book.

If you do not wish to be bound by the above, you may return this book to the place where you purchased it or to the publisher for a full refund.

Dedications

I dedicate this book to my kids Vikki, Harry and step son Jason; remember you can achieve anything if you put your mind to it. This book is proof.

My belated mother, my thoughts are always with you, I miss you dearly I know you would have been so proud.

My very patient loving wife Dolly who always supports me, in everything I do.

And lastly some notes of thanks

Richard Rains who I love like a brother, without his support in business and his belief in me, this book would have never been written.

Andrew Cross who's dedication to help me will never be forgotten.

And James Lavers whose immortal words still ring in my ears "dude you have to write a book" so I did.

hus•tle

1 [verb.] *Hustle*. A 'doer' who acts energetically and rapidly. Someone who jostles for position and makes it happen.

Foreword

You hold in your hands information that is a collection of my experiences, things I have learned over a quarter of a century, the things that I think have contributed to my success. Lessons that have moulded my behaviour and disasters that could have ended my career and, to be totally honest, unless you use it, all this is worthless and you might as well throw it in the bin and I really don't know why I bothered writing it! But seriously, if you do use it then it becomes absolutely priceless. Now I know that sounds like an outlandish statement but I have seen it happen. It happened to me. There are doers and donters (I had to add this word to my computer's dictionary as I made it up) in this life and I have to ask you: which one are you?

The biggest challenge that I find most investors come across is themselves and the fact you are reading this now puts you in a different class – a class above all the other so-called 'I want to do it' investors.

This industry is full of talkers; people tell me they want to be involved in property but never do anything about it.

I have written this book so you can see from my real life experiences how they can help you obtain your hopes, dreams and aspirations. Now I don't know everything but I do know what has and, more importantly, what has not worked. Because of the number of deals I have done and the dealings I have had with people, I'm well placed to share these experiences in order to help other like-minded people.

I did not get involved accidentally in teaching what I do; I did it because I have been very fortunate in my life to have been guided in a direction that enables me to have a fantastic lifestyle, and it's my hustling attitude that has brought this to fruition. Just as with this book you hold today.

I'm dyslexic and proud of it because that's the sort of determination that is required for success.

I wish you well in your pursuit of your dreams and until we meet.

Paul Ribbons

Contents

CHAPTER 1

Flipping for fun – My name is Paul Ribbons

And I trade houses for a living. My business partner and I buy properties off the open market; sometimes we may distress them, and then we sell them at auction for an instant profit. I'm a trader so I can't help but take the profit, because no matter how many houses you may want or own, unless you sell them or you own them outright you can't spend the rent or the equity (unless you want to keep borrowing against it).

Now I live for today, not in 35 years' time. I don't want a sports car when I'm 65; I want it now and why wait? I want massive income not passive income.

I have not worked full-time since 1996 and I have a lovely lifestyle. As I write this, I'm sitting on a balcony overlooking the Mediterranean Sea, and that's what it's all about to me – freedom and choices. Property gives me the things I want. In 1996 I sacked the boss and never looked back. It was scary at the time but I knew it was the right thing to do. You have to take risks in life if you want to get ahead.

Now ...

I'm going to assume something now and that's something I rarely do; I'm going to assume you're thinking about, about to or you are involved in property.

I have been involved in property for over 25 years now and I have worked through some really tough times. In that time, I have gained 12 years in total estate agency experience plus 15 years dealing and trading. I have also been involved with over 500 of what the industry calls 'below market value' (BMV) deals. So as you can see, I have had a little experience in this field.

In this book I'm going to reveal to you the most important things I have learned in my career over the last 25 years, how this has helped me and, more importantly for you, how this will assist you in your property business.

So let me ask you a question. Why property?

Now think about this for a moment as I find not many people do. I'm going to let you know why I got involved but before all that, let me tell you a story about a young guy.

He was talking with his dad and, whilst chatting, his father said, "How you are getting on at school?" The young guy showed him the league table of students in the whole school. The father was very surprised and said, "Well done son, I can't believe you're on top." "No dad, you have the paper upside down."

"Oh," he said, "that bad, huh?"

It was then that his father gave him some much-needed advice: "Look son, if you get into food, clothing or housing you will never be skint."

'Great advice' thought the son as he already had a job in a bakery at the weekends, so that was it. As for the other two, clothing did not interest him and housing was out of his league as, with no qualifications, that was going nowhere. So baking it was.

Now, after climbing to the heights of bakery manager this young man was ambitious and kept dreaming up lots of what his peers called 'pie in the sky' ideas. Every idea was poo-pooed by all the people he surrounded himself with.

But something was about to change, for as this young man at 23 years old realised, he had actually lived longer than his mother had (she was 23 years and 20 days old when she passed away) and it wasn't until he looked and said, "God, this was the message I could take from this tragedy; my mother gave me a gift and that gift was how precious life is." Every day after that day was a bonus so he made a decision that from then on he would not accept mediocrity and he would change things, starting right then.

The first thing was to buy a property, so off he went and bought one. Now, while buying it he built up a great rapport with the estate agent and, whilst it was not that apparent, this chance meeting would eventually change the direction of his life for ever. More of that later.

The second challenge was to change jobs; this was a little more difficult and needed some cunning strategies. Now he had spoken with the agent and asked, "How did you get into this business?" His reply opened up a whole new world. The agent said, "I used to be a Kwik-fit fitter." 'Bloody hell' thought the young man, 'they take anyone'. The agent then went on to say, "You have to have something about you as in this game it's very hard to crack it and many fall by the wayside."

"Oh, then do you think I should apply? I want to change my career and I'm very determined to get out of baking as there is not much dough in it."

"No," replied the agent, laughing at the poor attempt at a joke. But the seed was sown. What was on this young man's mind would not go away and he became obsessed with getting a job with an estate agent.

The next thing the young man did was invest in a suit, a briefcase and an Evening Standard (back in those days this was the main paper for London jobs).

Now I want you to think about this one for a few seconds. This guy had no qualifications whatsoever; who was going to take him seriously? And he buys a suit and briefcase! Anyway, the Evening Standard turned out to be a star buy. This proved to be fruitful as the young man noticed a job that seemed to suit him down to the ground. 'Manager wanted, no experience necessary'. He thought 'I'm a bakery manager, I could do that'. One phone call later and a date set for what was about to become the turning-point in his life. On the way to the interview, the young man popped in to see the agent whose office just happened to be on the way to the Tube (convenient).

The agent look startled. "Why the suit?" "I'm going for a new job, I did say I was determined." "Oh," sniggered the agent, "good luck." The young man sensed his lack of belief and this made him even more motivated.

Now we have to bear in mind the situation at this point: the baker from Walthamstow had just bought a house and racked up a £56k mortgage; this was sizable to someone on his salary.

And he had just exchanged contracts, so his timing was not the best. Also, with no education this seemed to anyone who spoke with him utter madness, but here's the thing: the job he was about to be offered was commission-only, selling insurance. Let me ask you a question: Would you take it on?

The equivalent mortgage today would be £200k.

Anyway, they offered him the job, he accepted and on the way back he popped in to see the agent again and said, "See, I told you I was going to change my career, I have just accepted this job, commission-only and I start in one week." The agent looked in total disbelief, rolled his eyes and shook his head and, instead of wishing him luck, said, "You're f***ing mad!"

The rest of his friends and family all said much the same, but he knew he could not accept mediocrity, or his mother's death when he was three years old would be all in vain.

Well, after two weeks' training he then contacted the agent to try and sell him some insurance. That was not his main reason for doing it although it did get him in front of the agent. When he turned up, he was greeted with rapturous laughter from all the staff, then he realised how much contempt they held for him. 'Never mind,' he thought, 'I will show them.'

Then it was into the office to meet Chris and Greg. Who was Greg? The area manager! This was unexpected and a great opportunity. The young guy started his pitch and Greg started to laugh and said, "Oh you're the one." "The one what?" the youngster replied. "You're this mad guy who's given up his job at the same time as taking on a large mortgage and all on a fat salary of zip." He explained to Greg as he had done to Chris that he had every intention of succeeding and that the idea that this was wrong never entered his head.

At that point the magical words were uttered, words that changed his life for ever.

Greg said, "You're either stupid or you have the biggest balls I've seen in a long while and you should be working for me." And that, as they say, is it; the rest is history.

The interesting thing for me is that this story is true and it's all about me, Paul Ribbons.

So why have I spent the last few pages telling you this story? Well, remember the question I asked at the beginning, this has everything to do with this.

Let me explain.

In order for anyone to succeed in anything you first have to know why you are doing it, because as one of my old mentors (Jim Rohn) said, "If you have a big enough why you will endure any how."

In other words, if what you want has enough emotion then you will do anything to get it.

I was prepared to suffer the consequences to get my hands on another job – financial ruin, even humiliation from my peers and the estate agents taking the piss.

So when you know why, then you have a foundation to work from.

I had a foundation and, more importantly, I had no idea what to do; this sounds strange but sometimes I believe that you can get caught up with the details.

I went into it knowing that I would succeed, full stop. All I had to do was figure it out on the way there.

I have read many books in the last few years and the most aptly-named book and the one that reminds me of this process is *Think and Grow Rich.*

Now I had a good reason for getting into property and it drove me a certain way forward, and it's interesting that whilst I had got the job I wanted, something was missing. I rose to become the manager and was being considered for further promotion but I was not fulfilling this burning desire within me. What I had noticed was the people I admired at the time were living a life very different from what I was experiencing. These people were driving flash cars, living in big houses, going on many luxury holidays every year and earning ten times what I was, for a fraction of the time spent.

I wanted a piece of that lifestyle. Let's be clear here; a life in property as an investor or developer/dealer is what I call Sexy – a lifestyle most people would envy. I did not envy it, I wanted it, full stop. I wanted to join those elite people I started to hang around with.

So I ask again, 'Why property?'

People business

I have been in the property business for over 25 years now, so I have gained a lot of experience, and valuable experience at that. My first ten years, as I mentioned earlier, were in estate agency; this was very valuable for my deal-sourcing skills. I went through the recession of the 90's which was very tough. I was good at agency and I was good because I had a great understanding of what I call the most important part of the property business – PEOPLE.

I have heard this cliché many times, 'I'm in the people business' but how many really understand this – I mean *really understand this?*

One of the reasons I'm deemed successful is because I really get this and it's been my greatest ally. When I first got into estate agency, Greg Georgiou told me something that stayed with me and will do for the rest of my life and this is it.

"95% of this business takes you two to five years to learn, depending on your capability. The other 5% takes you all your life to learn and that's people. Because we are all different and see things differently, we will always be learning from everyone."

One of the hardest things to do in any walk of life is to

put ourselves in someone else's shoes before thinking about ourselves. This goes against our natural instincts of survival but this is how I have negotiated some very tough deals. I need to know what's going on in the head of someone else before I can make any informed decisions, and this includes estate agents. This is why I have studied psychology and NLP, and obtained a coaching certificate, because I know and value this important subject.

I see many investors who state they understand this, although they never see it from any other perspective than their own. It's as if 'what's in it for me' takes over; they are stuck in what I call 'I-mode'.

How can this help?

A few questions I get asked regularly are:

1. Where does someone spot the deals? and

2. How can someone get started with no money?

In this book I will reveal to you all the system techniques and processes that have enabled me to source over 500 BMV deals In the last 15 years and also how I got started without a penny and, if these are carefully implemented into your property business, you can also yield spectacular results.

One client on my Flagship Reveal your Property Riches one-day event bought a house at 45% BMV to sell at auction; he made £22k on his very first deal. When I quizzed him on this he said that all he had done was to follow my strategy and the techniques I had taught him. He also followed the golden rules to enable him to do this.

NMD (No Money Down)

Back in 1996 I was a successful agent but I was restless; I was also going through a tough divorce and I had no money.

So if you remember the story I told earlier of how I got the job in the first place, you will know that I am rather determined. Also I wanted that lifestyle. So when I felt the time was right I made my move. I confronted my boss and we parted company on 21st February 1996. This was another turning-point in my life.

I did not know what was going to happen; all I knew was I could and would succeed.

I started to source properties for a select few developers that I had built good relationships with. I want you to bear in mind that I only deal with people I have 100% trust in, because when you start to source you are building rapport with agents and you need to know that whoever you pass it to won't mess it up. I know all too well that you only mess an agent about once, so make sure if you are sourcing for a third party you trust them. After about a year, one of the developers was a bit smart and said, "Why don't we team up in 50-50 partnership on any deals you find; your work and my money?" And he meant 50-50 win or lose.

We had been working together for a short while

when I came across a property that another dealer was selling; this is commonplace amongst traders as sometimes developers traded some houses rather than turn the deal away. This house was knackered and I thought we could get the works done for about £25k. Let's bear in mind that this was in 1996 and building costs were a lot lower, also we paid £40k for this wreck! I had complete control over what I purchased so I went and exchanged on the purchase prior to the building estimate. So when the building quote came in at £50k+ I felt ill. The house was only worth about £80k+ at the time, done up, so if we did the work and plus all the costs we were in for well over £95k – oops. I then realised what 50-50 meant; losses were not in my equations. So in a dilemma I had to go to my JV partner and say, "I have screwed up. What shall we do?"

Now I have to be honest, I did not expect the reaction I got. He said, "Never mind, a great learning experience and as long as you learn from it, we will be OK. I don't have to tell you what you did wrong, do I? We will place it in an auction and see how it fares; we have to guide it at £30k and with a reserve of £28k."

Now I was doing the maths and realised that I would have to stump up about seven to eight grand for my 50% so I was not pleased with myself, as you can well imagine. We placed it with Clarke Hillier's in early 1997.

On the day of the auction my little heart was pounding like mad. I was beyond nervous and what happened next sent me on a rollercoaster with my emotions. At first there were no bids and I thought 'Oh God' then someone shouted "20 grand" and the auctioneer took the maiden bid. It was like pulling teeth in this auction but at least we were off to a start. Now, my mind is very quick and I had already worked out that if it sold at early 20s we were in for £22k loss with cost. 'Oh shit, one of my very first deals and I'm already personally down £11k, and then there is My JV partner to consider, he will lose 11 grand also, all because of my stupidity of not doing my due diligence.'

I was once told luck is when opportunity meets preparedness; well my luck was about to change. I thought the hammer was about to fall at £25k but the bids just kept coming – 26, 27, 28, it got up to £40k and then I started to relax; 42,43,44 – it ended up at £52,750. Now that's a 32% increase – WOW!

Had I just invented BMV? Well, because out of necessity a strategy was born and that's what happened; everything either went into auction or was traded out to other dealers. Why do they work?

I had experienced some extreme emotions in that room and I realised people can't control their emotions in an auction, especially when its full of people, and this still works in any market – good or bad – as long as the property is deemed as cheap in the auction catalogue.

So the exit strategy was born and I have been doing this ever since: find a wreck and maybe distress it further, sell it via auction and away we go with the cash in our pockets.

CHAPTER 2

What makes a good deal

A few questions I'm asked regularly are how do I spot good deals and how much percentage do I look for BMV?

Now for a rant. I have quoted BMV because it's the industry measurement, but I do not like the term. What is below market value? It's below the price at which a RICS surveyor would value a property for mortgage purposes, at a level that the lender would lend, a price the surveyor thought it was safe for a lender to lend. What the surveyor would think a property should sell for.

Now my problem with this is that the surveyor is not an estate agent and would not know the accurate selling price. If the market is very strong then this value is around the value of the agreed price between seller and buyer, sometimes just behind. But when the market is weak the surveyor is usually very wrong because he uses out-of-date information. Just watch the stock market when there is uncertainty; values fall quickly and are volatile.

I'm a trader and I need facts not opinions, and that's what the surveyor's price is – an opinion.

So I have renamed BMV 'BSO': below someone's opinion.

So if I'm saying you can't trust a professional opinion, how do you ascertain a property's value?

This comes down to three things: what's for sale,

what's under offer and what's completed in the last three months. With this data I can work out what I think it will sell for, then I take 10% off this price; this figure I call FSV: forced sale valuation.

So as you can see, I take different information to work with and, with this in mind, I don't look for a percentage below FSV as I believe this restricts me to those parameters. The reason for this is simple: it stops me looking at a lot of the deals we have done and made good money on. Let me explain.

I agreed to buy a property in 2009; it was on the market for £70k; how much do you think I bought this house for? If it had been in tip-top condition it would have sold for £110k; it needed £25k spent on it and then I had my hidden costs, legals and all that jazz, so I would have been in for at least £30k in total.

If I paid £70k, this deal would be very tight, but here's the thing: I paid £75k. Now I know this would surprise a lot of people. How could I make it work? Well I understand some fundamentals and one of these is the law of supply and demand. Because at the time of buying this deal, the market was very strong for property that needed work, and because of the lack of supply this created a microclimate in the auction. And as sure as eggs are eggs, it sold for £88k; after costs it made £10k and we only owned it for two weeks in total.

So as you can see, the normal investor criteria does not apply here. Not all the deals I do fall into this formula.

As traders we are always looking to our market that we want to sell into and that's our barometer.

The thing is, most of the deals we do anyone could have bought; the trick is knowing what will turn a profit and what will not. Many of the investors I come across start to question me over deals they believe are great deals and ask me about putting them into auction. Because they think they have bought something that is what they consider to be 25% BMV (there it is again) or more, they feel sure they can sell it for more than they paid. What they do not realise is the auction market is full of people looking to add value, so an unmodernised property will sell well and a property in reasonable nick won't.

So now you know what will sell and you are crystal clear on who your buyers are, where do you start to look and what do you look out for?

THE MOST VALUABLE COMMODITY I KNOW IS RELEVANT INFORMATION

One of the most important things I have learned over the last 25 years is the importance of relevant information; the most valuable commodity I know is information.

I will give you an example.

Suppose you were offered a property; it was on the market for £150k and they were keen to sell it. You had arranged a viewing and as you were about to knock on the door I rang you and said the vendor had told me they would take £110k. Would this information influence how much you would offer? You are about to knock again and I ring to say that the vendor has only £50k mortgage and is not buying another property; would this change anything? And again you're about to enter and this time I ring to say the vendor is being repossessed in seven days and you have the cash to buy it. What happened? Did any of this information affect your decision? Of course it did, that's how powerful relevant information is. This one thing I got very early. Many sellers and agents try and keep certain information from you and it's my job to extract it.

Just imagine! A patient goes into the hospital with acute pains in the stomach, vomiting and looking very ill; the doctor looks for vital signs such as heart rate, temperature, blood pressure and colour of the skin. He would ask certain questions like, "What have you eaten and when did you last eat? Do you take any medication and do you have any known allergies?"

These questions and answers provide vital information in seeking a diagnosis so the doctor can decide what he will do next to treat the patient. He would not ask, "Where did you eat, what table did you sit at, was it a very nice meal, would you recommend it?" because that would be irrelevant information, wouldn't it?

I find that a lot of investors I come across are always trying to explain the vendor's circumstances, which are irrelevant. They may tell me that he's a nice guy, the wallpaper is green, he has lived there since the year dot, has seventeen brothers, and is very motivated because he's been on the market since March!

I go for three things when looking for information – it's like my vitals in the 'doctor' analogy:

What are the *Circumstances* (is he moving out and why is he moving out)?

Is the *Timing* right (does he need to move right away)?

And where is my *Leverage* (something I can use to get the price down)?

I call this procedure gaining ConTroL.

If I have no control then it is pointless me offering because, let's face it, the reason why any motivated seller would listen to a smart investor is that they have to because of their circumstances, and if they don't they are not even going to give you the time of day and you end up 'peeing' them off. More time is wasted on property where the vendor's position is not right or the timing is wrong and the investor has no leverage.

Once I spotted a property advertised on Rightmove; it had been on the market for about a month.

I'm looking for technical indicators and I had a few with this property: I noticed the picture was taken from the back of the house, the property was vacant and needed modernisation, and I did not recognise the agent from my normal search area.

When I teach this in my Flagship one-day event Reveal Your Property Riches, people are amazed at how much information they miss when I pull up a webpage such as Rightmove. When searching for properties on the web I look for three technical indicators:

1. I take a good look at the picture as this can give me lots of clues.

2. The text will reveal some great information.

3. If the agent is local or not (why would an agent out of the area sell a property?).

I noticed a particular property that was being dealt with by an agent out of town so I called to find out why he was advertising a property 50 miles out of his area. He said he was acting on behalf of the Official Receiver. This is such vital info as this property has to be sold, so we have a good indication that the circumstances are good.

As it had only been on the market for about a month, timing was a little weak but I decided to view it and called the agent to arrange a viewing. On arriving at the property, the agent was present with a locksmith. This is unusual considering it had been on the market for a month already. Now here's the thing: I was very interested in why the locks were being changed and the agent said that someone had super-glued the locks up. 'OK, that's feasible but not vital' I thought, so we viewed the property and all seemed to be OK.

Now I was not that strong on offering at this point

as I know most of the sales via these sources wait for some time before they take the sort of offers I want to pay; I was about £20k behind their price. What I needed was some serious leverage and my luck was about to change.

I called the agent the next day to discuss what could be done and I happened to mention the locks being changed and how this might be a problem. I was concerned by the fact it had been done once already; however the agent said no, the defaulting borrower had done it three times! Now this is vital. BINGO! A problem that won't go away because every time a viewing was booked the agent had to call a locksmith and this was costing him at least half a day in time plus the cost of a lock change and he was very pissed off!

At last I could get the leverage I wanted and after lots of to-ing and fro-ing and four months later (some deals can take time and patience is needed) I managed to buy it at £20k below the asking price. Great deal and it sold for a £10k profit.

Remember, relevant information counts for so much.

So what is ConTroL?

It's a combination of vital information. Can you see how that deal unfolded because I got the right information? I will be banging on about this all the way through the book, so be warned. ConTroL is the key to what I do and will unlock any deal if used correctly.

So as you can see, deals are not always easy to find; you have to look behind what might seem to be obvious.

Having been involved in hundreds of deals, I have learned that deals fall into a few certain categories.

Obvious deals

These are deals which are affected by condition or ones that need modernisation; it could be old-fashioned and even boarded-up. Structural problems, cracks in walls, sloping floors, bulging walls and sagging roofs – if the problem is obvious it's usually swarmed upon by everyone and his mother. This is what other developers, investors and dealers are after, and they are in big demand. These are difficult to gain control of unless you have good rapport with the agent or you happen to be in the right place at the right time.

I had a call once from a private seller; she was a little cagey with the info she gave me, she had a 'take it or leave it' attitude. As I always do with these calls, I booked a viewing. Now I have a few rules which I will cover later in another chapter and one is never assume anything. I did not want to assume it was a waste of time, because you never know. When I arrived it was obvious to anyone that this property had a major structural problem. In fact to this day I don't think I have seen any worse. The glass in the windows was split across the middle and caused by the movement in the building.

It's interesting how sellers can be quite casual about these types of things and she was trying to give the impression there was not much of a problem and tried to play it down.

Anyway I knew that it was worth money as a building plot and I priced it for that and proceeded to get as much info as I could; I needed control. We had leverage but because the vendor was playing it cool it was not as strong or in my favour as it could have been.

I kept asking questions regarding how many agents she had had out and if anyone else had tried to buy it, but to no avail. Now I was convinced that she had tried to sell it and she was still being very cagey. I said I would come back to her that afternoon as I had to do some figures. When I got home I did my due diligence and found it on an obscure auction site; I also knew the auctioneer and I called him, this auctioneer was not the strongest. They had tried to sell it at a much increased price and they had no bids. How much? £165k. I was thinking £125k. So I went back to the vendor and asked her about what I had found out. It was then she sang like a canary and told me she was desperate to sell and was concerned she would be there forever. She wanted to move near her son and her husband was poorly, so I got to the bottom of the situation. I said because she had exposed it via auction it had now caused a problem for me and I could only pay £125k; we agreed £125k and I sold it in a proper auction and made a £31k gross profit.

Now remember: ConTroL

The property had a problem but on its own it was not enough. I had to get the real circumstances and also timing, then the rest fell into place.

Another time I got a call from an agent to tell me that a property was coming to the market and no one had been in the house for about 20 years. It was a probate and had to be sold to pay inheritance tax. Now when I hear this I get excited because you can guarantee it will be a dump and I love dumps. Sure enough it was.

The agent would not even go inside and admitted she thought it was haunted. Great, OK, I will go in and have a look. I have to admit I was a little spooked but I was far too proud to show it. The property was so overgrown that I took me 20 minutes to get in. Now this got me thinking 'Had she been in at all and if not who had?'

No one; she just assumed it needed everything doing and valued it as such. Because she had not viewed she had not seen the extension at the rear which would increase its value substantially. Even the solicitor advised the agent not to go in because of the property being haunted. This was great news for me. All I had to do was give my offer based on how bad the property was because no one was about to check. Also the agent did not want to keep coming back to 'that house' so leverage all the way.

Another thing was interesting; inheritance tax only kicked in at the time around the £300k mark, so the vendor could have been left a lot of assets because why would she have to sell a property quickly in order to pay tax? Sure enough, there were others and we bought another one, we made £100k out of those two deals just by asking the right questions and having the right information.

So I want more information.

The next category: Non-obvious

This is where your skills will be needed. When I was an agent we used to have a saying 'A property is not a deal until it has been aborted three times,' in other words, if a property has had three buyers fall through and the same problems come up then it will usually be ripe for picking up at the right price. Spotting these can be a bit tricky and a great follow-up system is required in your business to identify these.

There are lots of things to look out for, like no planning permission on extensions and loft conversions, any works carried out without building consent, flats with short leases, Japanese Knotweed, title problems, previously underpinned property – there are so many.

I was trawling the net once and I came across a property which was clearly a repossession. It had been on the market for some time and I noticed that there had been numerous offers on it. I called the agent to gain some info and he told me that there was a problem: the property had Japanese Knotweed growing in the garden. This causes an issue with lenders as they define it as un-mortgageable. The lender was panicking as it was spring and they were worried that it could spread. They were so worried they instructed a company to eradicate it. The only thing with this was it takes three years to die off and while it's still there it's an issue with mortgage companies.

I offered on this property three times and eventually got it for £90k; its original asking price was £139k. It sold it at a profit of £26k. I knew it would not affect a cash buyer in the auction and so took the gamble.

Because they are not blatantly obvious, you have to enquire; I always ask agents if they have any properties that have problems.

I was speaking with an agent about a property and whilst talking with him I asked if he had any others which were problems. He said, "I do have one with a really short lease but you won't want it as it's virtually unsalable."

Here the thing – everything is sellable at the right price. So I asked how long the lease was and he replied, "21 years." Great, I needed to find out by how much the freeholder wanted to extend the lease as this would be the basis of my offer. The freeholder was in cuckoo-land and wanted far too much. Now this gave me leverage on the seller, as unless either the vendor or a buyer wanted to go through the process of arbitration, then that was the only figure I could work with despite his protests.

So I agreed to purchase it for £50k. Flats in general good condition were selling at the time for £165k and the freeholder wanted £65k to extend the lease, plus the flat needed full modernisation. That was another

£40k including costs, so this was not the bargain of the century. What I do understand though is when something goes to auction looking so cheap it usually attracts lots of interest.

And it just so happened to attract so much interest it sold for £96,500. Now that did surprise me as I only expected £65k.

Adding value

Another way we have benefited from dealing is to spot properties where you can add value. Some of the best ones have been properties where very few alterations are needed, small changes in layout, also extensions, corner-sited, conversion-potential building plots.

When searching the net over a period of several weeks I noticed a studio flat. Now I have a phobia with studios as, when the market is poor, they don't sell well and lenders get very nervous about them. I thought I would view this one as it was a little expensive but the market was strong at the time. But it had not sold over a period of months and also it was a period studio. I called the agent and asked if he knew when it was converted or how long the lease was (this would give me an indication as to how long was left on the lease). It had a 79-year lease so it was probably converted 20 years previously. I felt it was worth a view as some of the older conversions were very poorly laid-out, they were done on the cheap. I also knew that type of property would normally convert into 1 bedroom and the layout of houses in that street indicated to me something could be done.

When I got there, my gut reaction was 'right, a poor conversion' where the dimensions were lounge/ bedroom 15x11, kitchen 10x9 and bathroom 10x9. All that had to be done was split the kitchen into a separate bathroom and kitchen and turn the bathroom into a bedroom. I agreed to buy it and flipped it as soon as I had exchanged to another dealer who was looking for a one-bed to refurbish. I showed him what he could do and he gave me a profit of £15k. It just goes to show – on the market for months and no one else saw it.

I got a call once from an agent who had a two/three-bedroomed house on the market. I send reminders to agents to keep my details fresh in their minds. This agent said the property needed modernisation and was a little bit expensive and thought I would not buy it. I don't like agents to think for me because I need to make the decision, not them. Anyway I went to view and saw straight away that it could be altered. I did not let the agent know my thoughts; instead I said, "Bid the asking price," and she nearly fell on the floor.

It was laid out as a two/three bedroom but the staircase was on the same side as the rear addition so it would be easy to put a partition the length of the room to make it independent. Also the room that was created could be split into two rooms: a bathroom and a separate bedroom. In that area, if a property has three bedrooms and an upstairs bathroom they sell for a lot more than two beds with the bathroom off a bedroom.

This was all well and good but how could I get my buyers to see this? Once exchange had taken place I committed it to auction and, before any viewings took place, I marked out the floor with the upside-down spray paint you get from the builders' merchant, to show what could be done.

This was a real winner; it sold and made a £26k profit, all because I could see what could be done.

Undervalued properties

Let me ask you a question.

Let's say there are two identical houses, one has been lived in by an old lady who has kept it clean and tidy, it looks immaculate and you could live there if you needed to. The property is generally old-fashioned, all the ceilings have tiles and both bathroom and kitchen were replaced in the early 1980s. It has central heating installed and has hardwood and aluminium double glazing.

The second one has been neglected; it needs everything doing including kitchen and bathroom, all the ceilings have fallen in and it looks a complete mess. It has no heating or double glazing.

Which one's worth more?

Now when we compare these houses, most people would assume that the property which is clean and tidy will sell for more. But here's the thing; they both need the same amount of work to bring them up to date. Even if a property has central heating fitted in the early 1990s it will be so inefficient it needs replacing.

So they are worth the same.

Some agents get this very wrong.

It never ceases to amaze me how agents still don't get values right. The number of times I see property come to the market where there is a bidding frenzy and the agent ends up getting substantially more for it. Then I hear them say, "This is ridiculous, that property is not worth anywhere near that." This is someone who does not clearly understand the laws of supply and demand. There is and has always been demand for property that needs modernisation, and a house is always worth exactly what someone is willing to pay for it.

But I'm not going to complain as it has been to my favour. I would say anything I have bought and made a profit on probably has been undervalued but sometimes it is more obvious than others. I regularly pay more than the asking price if I can see a profit.

I can recall a property that came on to the market; the agent thought I was going to offer what he thought was a silly price. This property was so smelly it made you want to retch; you know when someone tells you not to smell something because it's so bad, but you have to and, when you do, you start to gag and you can't wait to get some fresh air. It was that bad!

It was a repossession and the company had to get it fumigated first because of the flea infestation. The defaulting borrower had kept cats in there and was afraid they would run away so she never let them out; there was cat mess everywhere. I'm feeling quite ill thinking about it.

Anyway this came to market and the agent did not want to go in. I, on the other hand, knew this was undervalued because all it needed was a professional clean. The agent had only seen a disaster and never saw past that.

The asking price was £42k and there was lots of interest; the agent thought I would be offering very low, about £35k. What happened next shocked her; I offered £55k. I knew it was worth £65k+ in the room and I had to knock everyone else out. My tactic worked and I then sold it for £70k. Now this is happening all the time; even at the time of writing this book we are negotiating something that's above asking price. I would say 15% of the properties I deal with I'm offering between 5-10% above asking price. I do appreciate that this is hard for people to do and you have to be very disciplined to do it.

Grossly over-inflated values

This category fascinates me. It's about psychology because the asking price is not always the right price. I know this as an ex-estate agent. Now when I was selling houses I would never take on a property unless I had a good chance of selling it. Some vendors want to try a silly price before they will take an offer and if

I know this I would consider taking the instruction.

This is where I score regularly; I look out for these and do you remember ConTroL? Because I have this firmly in mind, if I can see all these in play I will offer, because you never know.

This happened recently; a house came to the market and you could not see this house at all and that's what drew me to it. It had three conifer trees in the front garden and the house was covered in ivy. Now when I say 'covered' I literally mean covered – the windows and the roof. There was no natural light getting to the house. Now for a big tip: if you want to find out if the price is what the vendor is hoping for or what it is the agent valued it at, ask this question: "Is this your price or the vendor's price?" This gives the agent a chance to let you know whether he thinks it's a ludicrous price or not.

That's what I asked him when I enquired about it. Right on cue he said, "Well it's what the vendor wants to try." I could deduce from this that the agent had taken on this instruction on the basis the vendor would accept a much lower figure. Also, because of the state of the property I could feel confident that the environmental department from the council was putting pressure on the vendor to either clean it up or sell it. It was on the market for £120k at that time and we were buying houses in that location for £70-£80k. Now I'm always thinking about ConTroL so I wanted to find out about the circumstances. I asked the agent if he knew of any impending orders from the council, also if the neighbours had given the vendor any grief.

He did not know.

So I called the council and they confirmed that an environmental order would be issued if the vendor did not take some sort of action. BINGO, some leverage. I went to view and the property also suffered from the ivy internally; the roots had grown through the walls into the basement – more leverage.

I got this property for £62k, that's nearly half its asking price. This is funny; some people would think the asking price is the value. I have another golden rule – Ignore the Price – and that's why.

And I had a big helping hand the day of the auction because lots of investors had seen it on the open market at £120k; when it went into the catalogue it looked cheap. I guided it at £55-£65k and it looked cheap (even though it wasn't) and it sold for £101k. Yippee!

Timing

Now this category is very important as timing can be everything. It also covers a lot, from being in the right place at the right time through to being very quick to make a bid before everyone else gets there.

And that reminds me of a property that came to market a while back. I was trying to get in with a particular agent and knew they had access to some very old stock through an old management company. Anyway I used some tools on Rightmove to alert me to new properties coming on to the market. On this particular morning, it was a Friday, a property came through that was on with the agent I was trying to get in with. It looked cheap, it was an ex-rental and at the time it was under £100k – £96k to be precise. I called the agent immediately and she said, "Not you as well, everyone and his dog wants to see this." "OK, when can I see it?" I asked. "Monday is the earliest." "Is there any chance I could see it before?"

Now for another Ribbons top tip: don't take no for an answer. Because she said no, I then asked, "Is there any way I could see it at any time before Monday?" "No," she said. Now I'm like a little kid and those of you who have kids will understand what I'm on about. I then asked, "Why?" She then said, "The tenants are moving out today and they will be cleaning it tomorrow, I don't work Sundays so Monday is the earliest and I have 25 viewings for it at 12." What she did not realise is that I'm very tenacious and I keep going. So I decided to pay a visit to the property and, sure enough, the tenants were moving. Now I'm a very helpful chap and asked the tenants if I could help them with their heavy boxes. They said, "Yes please," and when I finished helping them I asked if I could look around. They obliged and I went back to the agent within two hours and offered the asking price. I got the property before anyone else, and the agent saved herself the hassle of viewings on the Monday.

Remember, the most valuable commodity I know is info. If I had not pressed the agent I would not have found out that information, but most importantly I dropped everything I was doing to get round there and bought a cheap house. We went on to sell it for £113k – £17k gross profit for getting my timing right.

Cool.

The number of investors I see chasing properties where the timing is all wrong; if a property comes to the market, unless it's cheap and undervalued in the first place, you are wasting your time.

I had a call from an agent once who understood this principle well.

Sometimes outside forces can help you out and on this particular property Lady Luck was smiling, as she often does for me. The Olympic bid had been secured by London and people started to get what I call 'Stratforditus'; it seemed very infectious.

His vendor had three sales fall out of bed. Remembering the advice I had been given many years earlier about a property not becoming a deal until it's been aborted three times, I started to get excited and I also knew his office was in Stratford. The vendor wanted to go into a warden-assisted flat and the property she was buying was about to be put back on the market. She did not want to lose out so she asked the agent what he would suggest. He said that cash buyers were an option but she would get less and, if she wanted, he could get a couple round to see if the price might be acceptable. I went round and used my 'seven stages to negotiation' technique (I will go through that later and it's powerful!). Because she wanted peace of mind I bought the property for £215k and she had sold it three times at £250k. Now the bonus was my buyer had caught Stratforditus and he was a dealer and paid me £250k cash and completed in my shoes; in other words we did not have to complete ourselves, we used the buyer's money.

As you can see, there are many categories here and these are the main ones. I could spend a lot more time on this, as over the last quarter of a century I have come across many different situations. As we progress through this book, other examples are going to pop up and you will have even more situations to look out for.

This next chapter is solely how to spot deals on the open market with estate agents and you will see how the above categories fall into place.

CHAPTER 3

How to spot deals on the open market

It's amazing to see people's mouths drop and the 'ah-ha moments' people get on my Flagship Reveal Your Property Riches one-day event.

What I'm going to show you here is so simple you won't look at a webpage the same way ever again.

I'm going to start with my seven steps to finding deals.

1. Have strict criteria

When looking for anything, whether it's a car or a house, you have to have an idea of what you want. Imagine looking for a car with no specific idea of what you want. What sort of car do you need? Is it for a family or a young couple with no kids? Do you want a four-door saloon, five-door estate, three-door coupé, two-door sports convertible, 4X4, small car, big car? And so you get my drift. Well, houses are very much like this: is it a terrace, end terrace, semi-detached, house, flat or bungalow? See what I mean, where do you start? Most investors are looking for investments, which is fine, but how do you spot investments?

There needs to be something more specific to find great deals; I see investors travelling the country chasing investments that return them good yields. On Rightmove at any one time there are over 880,000 properties for sale in the UK alone and that's just one website. So you have heard of the saying 'it's like finding a needle in a haystack'.

Now I don't know about you, but I get overwhelmed

very easily and, being dyslexic, I tend to throw my toys out of my pram. When I was a kid they used to call me lazy. I prefer to call myself ruthlessly efficient; I want to find the fastest and most efficient way of doing something.

My criteria are simple: un-modernised, two/three-bed terraced houses up to £100k, in certain areas.

So to be clear and remember 'clarity is power' (Tony Robbins):

1. The unit

2. The price

3. The area

Once you have that sorted and clear, it's time to move on to Number Two.

2. Have the right tools and a system for follow-ups

Stick to one:

1. Website – Rightmove

2. Tool – Property-bee

3. Follow-up system

Now this may seem a little obvious, but the use of the correct tools is essential.

I use Rightmove as the main search website for properties. I shall make this crystal clear: every decent agent I know has all their properties on Rightmove. It's the most powerful property website out there.

I like searching on Rightmove; I can flick through page after page quickly and effectively. But when I spot something that needs more information, there is a tool that I highly recommend. That tool is Property-bee and it gives me information as to when the agent first put it on Rightmove and all the alterations that an agent makes during its time on the website. So what I do is search without Property-bee first then switch over once I have identified a potential deal.

Another system I use in my business is follow-ups. This one thing has earned me so much money it's ridiculous. 30% of all properties that agents agree with potential buyers fall through – 30%!

I always follow up on these types of properties. Anything on Rightmove that meets my criteria and with a green sticker showing SSTC, SOLD or UNDER OFFER I'm all over like a rash. I'm looking for information and if it's early days I put it to a system to follow up in a designated time frame.

Another good reason to follow up is you are constantly in the agent's mind. If you phone every week to follow up on a property, you will be speaking with this agent and if that company is the type of firm to get deals they may have more.

50% of the deals I do are from my follow-up folder. If this is the only thing you take from this book you will increase your chances of buying deals ten-fold.

I remember chasing a property that was under offer. I called the agent every single week to ask him how his sale was progressing. At first he was polite; after a few more weeks he started to get rude. He would say things like, "Paul, I've told you I will call you if it falls through." Now I know the chances of him calling me are about 50/50. That is not enough of a chance so I kept calling. I don't care if he gets pissed off, I will keep chasing it until it's dead (exchanged with someone else) or I get my own way. He got so pissed off he actually said, "For God's sake, are you deaf?" "No," I replied, "just very tenacious."

It was after 12 weeks that I got my own way. The other party had stil not exchanged, so I mentioned that I could do the deal with a faxed contract with a conditional exchange subject to a local authority search. Eventually the agent let me have a crack at it and we did exchange in 24 hours.

But here's the thing, that persistence paid off big time, this agent had never sold anything to me up until that stage. He even admitted to me afterwards that he thought I was a bit of a Messer – that's estate agent talk for investor. I have received many deals after that because he can trust me, he knows I will do the deal. Now he calls me first and when he puts my offer forward, he does so with absolute conviction.

Now you have the startings for the next step.

3. Search

- Photo

- Text

- Agent

This is where the fun begins for me as I love poking around on Rightmove.

If you keep in mind the saying I have for information *'The most valuable commodity I know is information'*, it's most important at this stage. This is the embryonic stage where I first notice things and I'm looking for what I call 'technical indicators'.

So what are technical indicators? As I mentioned before, they are little pieces of info that lead me to deals. It is surprising how little info you need to spot an opportunity.

So the first element to look for is the photography.

This can tell me a lot about the vendor and could lead to revealing the circumstances. Imagine seeing a kid's bike on the front lawn and the grass is growing through the spokes; what does this tell you? I would make enquiries about this property because if a vendor can't look after their kid's bike, what else do they neglect? And remember at this stage I'm looking for clues, it's like browsing.

So what else do you need to look out for?

I would ask you to look at this picture and see if you can spot anything about it. I will say there are plenty of clues if you look carefully.

The fact it has double yellow lines outside tells me it's a main road. Also below the front window there is some cracking to the brickwork, this could lead to a deal in itself.

The next thing I'm interested in is the text; this can give us some good clues again. And sure enough it mentions needs modernising and also it has a short lease.

But the most important thing on this page is something that hit me as soon as I looked at it; it struck me and had me calling the agent immediately, something that led to a potential deal.

It was that the agent advertising this property was in a totally different location from the property. Now

I have to ask the question, 'Why would an agent at least 60 miles away from the property be instructed to sell it?'

My phone call proved lucrative as they had been given the instruction from an insolvency practitioner. These properties are actually better then repossessions as I find the firms are more aggressive and want them sold quickly.

As you can see, there is information that helps you to spot deals all the time if you have your eyes open.

So once you have identified a potential deal, how do you get the information that helps you to buy the deal?

This brings us nicely to our next step: call the agent to get as much information as possible.

4. Call the agent

- Circumstances

- Timing

- Leverage

Do you remember what I said about ConTroL:

'It's the circumstances that reveal the opportunities that lead to deals.' Paul Ribbons

When I spot a potential property, the very first

question I ask is, "What are the circumstances?' By asking this question first, I save myself lots of time because if the circumstances are wrong what will be the point? Even if you have leverage does not mean they will take a Paul Ribbons bid.

I have questions and ways to reveal the answers I want.

One way is to ask the agent, "What are the circumstances of the vendor?"

If this does not reveal it, then I ask, "Why is the vendor selling?"

Now sometimes it's obvious, like a repossession or a probate. The ones I am more interested in are the ones where people have moved out. If you ask the right questions, it should reveal some interesting facts. If they have moved out, did they buy something else or are they renting? Why would someone leave a property empty and then go into rented accommodation?

I remember dealing with one of my mentees recently. He had seen a property and I asked him what the circumstances were. He explained that the vendor was moving out and there was no chain. He thought this was enough information. I wanted more: "Why is the vendor moving out?" After pressing the agent they told him that the vendor was going into rented because the guy lived in a four-storey house and he was struggling with the stairs. Now this sounds feasible, doesn't it?

I was not convinced; again why would someone who clearly bought a house with four floors in the first place give up his home and certainty for a rented bungalow? I pressed for more info; let's view the house and speak to the vendor. On the viewing, I asked the vendor, "Why do you want to go into rented accommodation when you have a comfortable home and your husband could live on one floor?"

Then she revealed the information I was looking for, the real circumstances and leverage. Her husband had become disabled in the last few months and had to give up work; this was causing financial pressure and they had to move or face financial ruin. They had missed mortgage payments and could not get a mortgage for another house so they had to sell. Herein this gives me all the info I need, all because I would not accept someone's word for it. Can you see how easily that info could have been missed?

It certainly pays to question what people say. I have another rule and that's never rely on what you are told.

I'm also looking for Timing; now the timing was not right for that vendor, they did not have enough pressure at that time although six months later my client bought it.

Now I said I was going to bang on about ConTroL and I meant it because the next step is the Viewing which I sort of covered in this last example, but there is more to it than that if I want ConTroL.

5. The Viewing

- Circumstances

- Timing

- Leverage

So what do I look for on the viewing? I'm checking the circumstances because I know people don't always tell the truth. It's OK if the vendor lives there, I can normally get to the bottom of it. But what if the property is vacant? I will have to question the agent at the property, asking him again to confirm what the circumstances are.

I'm also looking for Leverage, some sort of fault to use to get the price down.

Things I look for are neighbouring houses; they can hold a property's value back as it puts buyers off.

I'm on the lookout for any structural weakness, like cracks and sloping floors, or other things that could add value.

I make a list of all the works to be carried out. It's as if I need to find something to bring the price down or something that makes me want to buy it.

Also its location is vital, so remember the old cliché: 'Location, Location, Location'. You can always change a property's facade and you could rebuild it, but you can never replace its location.

I remember going to view a property in the summer

of 2009. I had just bought a new motorbike and I received a call while I was out for a ride. I explained to the agent that I was out riding on my bike and asked if it was OK with the vendor if I turned up in leathers. As I expected, he was OK with it. When I turned up at the property he was waiting outside to greet me. He advised me to lock up my bike because people might nick it. I said, "It's insured, don't worry." This property's location was not great and I thought 'this is a good start' as the vendor was already on the back foot, admitting it was not a good area. Anyway I went in to view his house. Now I'm always looking for leverage and his house was very smelly and I love smelly houses, but it was not enough to get it for the price I wanted.

It's interesting how people see things sometimes, I was lucky this time and for all the wrong reasons. I looked around the house, making a mental note of all the faults and, when I looked out of the window, my bike had in fact been nicked. This guy went mental. How could they do this? I did remind the fella that he had warned me to lock it up and all the time I'm thinking it could not have been better timing. The thing is, when I bought the bike the garage had warned me this might happen so I got them to fit a tracker. The vendor offered me a lift and while in the car he told me that this was the reason he wanted to move. His wife could not stand it anymore. I told him I was not sure if I wanted to buy the house because if they kept nicking things it would be hassle. He said, "Come on, there must be a price that you would pay." I replied, "Yes, but you won't like it." He said, "Well what is it?" As soon as he said that I knew the deal was mine. By the way, the police found the bike one hour later.

We paid £67k and sold it after a good professional clean for £100k and I got my bike back unmarked. Not a bad day really.

So if you see enough houses like I do you will come across all sorts. The viewing is essential, not for whether you want to buy it or not but for gathering information – the most valuable commodity I know.

Once you have all this information the next is you.

6. Due diligence

- For sale

- SSTC

- Completed sales

I have been dealing and valuing property for some 25 years and I'm fascinated by how little due diligence people do, or how over the top people go.

I see people paying for complicated reports like Hometrack which to me are a complete waste of time. It's not real time, it looks at info that's out of date and is irrelevant to investors, developers and traders like me. Remember I renamed BMV 'BSO' and that's all it is – someone's opinion.

Two things are needed to make a more accurate assessment of a property's true value: what comparables (comps) are on the market today and how long have they been on? This gives me a snapshot of what the market is doing right at this moment in time. You could have lots of comps of sold property but if the market is slow then this will show up. I look for properties that have been on for a while and why they have not sold. I need facts, not fiction.

It's interesting that, in our experience, when there is weakness in the market prices can drop by 10% if you need to sell quickly, so always look for weakness in the market. And this could be caused by a number of different things. I remember in July 2007 interest rates were raised to 5.75%; at the time, this was the height of the boom cycle. At the next auction we saw values slip because there was a sharp intake of breath as the market digested the news. What did this mean? Were rates going further and how is this going to affect yields? Confidence gets knocked. That was the start of the decline, but if you listen to the news they will tell you it was the recession of 2008. It's funny – as a trader you get to see what's happening well before everyone else.

Now because of this insight we can predict values to a certain degree.

The next comparables to look for are properties that are under offer. What sales have been agreed and, more importantly, how long were they on the market beforehand? Again, this gives a snapshot of what's going on. Big tip coming up.

If you want to find out what a property has sold for, don't ring up and just ask the agent as they will not tell you. Ring up and say you are from outside the area and you need to get some comparables on properties in the area and could they offer you any. Don't tell them you're an investor; let them think you're a property professional like a surveyor and they will normally give you the information you need. I actually say I'm a surveyor from out of the area and no agent has ever asked me what company or anything to prove it. They always give me the info. Cool!

Now it's time to have a quick peek at completed sales. Use Rightmove sold prices which are the same as the land registry information. This is where caution is necessary as the info could be well out of date. It's already a minimum of three months out of date. How long does the average transaction take to go through? In my experience, it's six to nine months from start to finish so some of this data could be up to a year old. I only look to give me comfort on the other information I'm getting.

Can you see how all this information falls into place?

So now it all comes together and this leads to Step Seven.

7. Getting ready for negotiation

At this stage I check everything before I arrive at a price I want to pay.

- Have I got ConTroL?

- Have I done due diligence?

And then I ask my vital questions

- My questions

1. Do I want this?

2. Is there demand for it?

3. What will it sell for?

4. What do I want to pay?

5. If I have to, will I pay more?

Then I apply golden rule number four which is: if I think of the figure I want to offer I then take off 10%; that's the price I want to pay.

Once I have the figure I want to pay and I'm clear on if I will pay more, it's time to negotiate.

I have a lot to say about this in another chapter.

CHAPTER 4
Paul's Rules

I'm a very fortunate man; I have the benefit of hindsight.

Tony Robbins says:

'Success is the result of good judgement, good judgement is the result of experience and experience is the result of bad judgement.'

Now I think never a truer word has been spoken because I have made some spectacular mistakes. I find this quite refreshing – someone admitting that they mess up.

Not every deal wins and yes the Charlie Big Bananas Paul Ribbons screws up and has done many times. It's OK to mess up now and again, but what you learn from it is what counts for so much.

Another saying is *'The definition of insanity is doing the same thing time and time again and expecting a different result.'*

So I have compiled a list of rules in order to help you become more successful in property.

I'm going to start with my Five Golden Rules:

1.   NEVER ASSUME ANYTHING

2.   NEVER RELY ON WHAT YOU'RE TOLD

3.   ALWAYS IGNORE THE PRICE

4. NEVER OFFER THE PRICE YOU WANT TO
    PAY; TAKE 10% OFF

5. NEVER GET EMOTIONAL ABOUT STOCK

Rule No. 1: Never assume anything

It's interesting how this rule came about; the thing is, this has been with me for most of my life and is part of my own personal philosophy.

If you think about it in your own life, how many times do we assume things? Sometimes it's difficult not to.

I remember a couple of deals that I have done where this rule came in very handy and explains the importance of it.

I had a call from a private advert I placed in the local paper. The advert was placed in the Medway edition and the caller was from south-east London. He spoke with a very strong and exaggerated Cockney accent and I thought it could be one of my mates mucking about. They sometimes used to ring up pretending to be a punter with a cheap house to wind me up. After some questions I thought he could be genuine, so I booked an appointment; I always book an appointment because you never know where it could lead. He was pressing me on what percentage I would offer him of his initial asking price. I do not commit to this on the phone and would rather talk to him face-to-face. So I booked an appointment and arranged it on my way to Bluewater shopping centre with my wife.

On my way there I kept thinking this was a waste of time and, as we went past the shopping centre, I said to my wife, "I think this will be a waste of time, shall I ring him and cancel?" She looked at me with a puzzled look in her eye. I said, "What's up, babes?" She replied, "Since when have you started to assume things, as you always tell me nothing is a waste of time?" "Pardon?" I said (I'm not used to people questioning me). She said, "You heard me the first time. In all the time I have known you up until now you have never assumed anything and you would bash the kids about it, me about it and even yourself. You are proud to never assume anything."

Now I'm not used to having my tail between my legs and my wife does not normally interfere with business but she had a point. Gingerly, I agreed to go and see it, and lucky I did.

I turned up a little early. The guy had said he was on nights and would not be in before 12. While waiting outside, I was not getting a good feeling and it was out of our territory at the time. Then I spotted a guy who looked like he had fallen out of a skip; I thought to myself 'I bet that's him' and I knew it was a waste of time. It was him and he was a very polite fella. Anyway I went in and the flat was immaculate; it was on the market for £200k, I wanted to pay £160k max. Now, as you will learn in this chapter, I think of a figure and take off 10%; this time I rounded it off to £150k. When I offered this he asked, "How quickly can you do it?" I said, "Tomorrow," and the funny thing was we sold it prior to auction at £175k. I never did say 'thank you' to my wife for that valuable lesson.

Another time I was visiting an agent in my local area. He said there was a property not far from my home and it was on two titles, one being the house with a small garden, and the other three acres of land at the rear. Also, on the land at the rear the vendor was keeping chickens, geese, horses and cows; she had agreed to buy a property in Norfolk and needed to sell very quickly.

The agent explained to me he thought the beauty of the deal was in the land at the rear. Now I wanted to get in the agent's good books and also I was thinking to myself 'this is a waste of time' because the property was too expensive and she needed the money from this house to buy the next one. Also the land at the rear was green belt and the local authority would not grant planning permission.

But I remembered that nothing was a waste of time and I cannot assume anything so I went along. I did explain to the vendor I was a dealer and looking to make money but felt that I could not get planning for the three acres. She thanked me for my honesty and said her neighbour had been turned down for the same thing. Now two things happened when I spoke with her: she knew that I knew what I was talking about and I was honest.

But the best was yet to come. As I was leaving, she said, "Do you buy anywhere?" "Yes, of course we do, why?" I replied. "Well, my father died last year and left me a house in SE6 and it's a bit of a mess."

She also told me she had called National Home Buyer Man – a company advertising on national TV. I knew they would offer less then I would, so all I had to do was be higher than them. I bought that house for £131k and sold it at auction for £175k, all because I did not assume anything.

£69k from two deals – that's a rule worth having.

Rule No. 2: Never rely on what you are told

I visited a mate of mine who I used to work with many years ago; he was an agent in Stratford. He had a huge whiteboard in his office where they used to post their new instructions and on the board was a house described as three flats with no planning. I asked him if it was any good for me and he said no as they wouldn't grant planning in that area any more. The local authority insisted that properties had to be a certain size to convert. Now, as the rule suggests, I'm not one for accepting what people tell me so I asked for an appointment.

The vendor was an old Jamaican fella and I asked how long this had been three flats. He replied, "Since 1962 when my father came over." Now all I had to do was prove this had been three flats and I could get what they call a Certificate of Lawfulness. If a property has been converted for a certain length of time then you can apply for this but you have to have proof. I asked the vendor if he would put that in writing but he refused because he did not want to get into trouble with the local authority. Despite my assurances that they could do nothing about this, he said no.

So I agreed to buy it from him but I knew the value was in the Certificate of Lawfulness. I left the appointment and this was my mission – to prove it had been three flats for more than ten years.

The first place I looked was the Council Tax department. I asked them if they could tell me what the Council Tax banding was for the property; they replied, "Is that flat A, B or C?" 'Brilliant' I thought. I asked them if they could put that in writing and they said if I could prove I was the owner they would, otherwise no. Oh shoot, I have to buy it first to find out and that's risky. The next place I tried was the services: gas, electric and water. The trouble with that was people change their energy suppliers nowadays more often than they change their underwear, so no joy there. In the end I gave up and thought 'Sod it, I can't be bothered.'

You don't believe I would do that, do you? Well I didn't, as I do not give up! And then I had a great idea. When Council Tax first came in, in 1993, the district valuer's office was responsible for valuing every property in England, so I rang their office and they said, "Is that flat A, B or C?" I asked if they could put that in writing and they said, "Of course." It's interesting how one department says no and another says yes. This information was very valuable as I had an investor who paid us a £50k clear profit because he had Stratforditus and he wanted flats in that area. All because I don't rely on what people tell me.

I remember being contacted by an auctioneer and they

had a property they could not put to auction because the vendor was being repossessed before the auction date and the auctioneer's office was trying to help the vendor. Her house had burnt down but because her husband who had left her six months earlier had got them into arrears, the building society had cancelled their insurance and never reinstated it, so there was no insurance policy to claim on. She had an £82k mortgage secured against it and the auctioneer said that they had to get £85k to cover the mortgage and fees.

Lots of people had been to see the house and all sorts of figures were being offered from £60k up to £75k. This house had no roof and the whole of the first floor was gone.

I had arranged to meet the vendor at the property. She had four kids and had to go into emergency accommodation and she had broken her leg trying to get her kids out of the burning building. The auctioneer was adamant it had to be £85k and was appalled at all the prices that were being offered. The vendor has remained a firm friend of mine since this tragic event. I was very sympathetic to the situation but a property is only worth what it is worth, I'm not in it for charity.

Now I have this rule, as you know, and I was racking my brain on how to do this deal. This deal was not about the price the vendor wanted, it was about how much the building society (BS) wanted to clear the outstanding mortgage and they were putting on pressure which I felt was unjust and unnecessary, especially with the circumstances of the woman and her kids.

I spoke to the auctioneer and suggested to him he speak to the BS to see if there was any movement on the final price. He was not very responsive, suggesting to me that I did not understand the full implications of his client's predicament. He was very posh and had an air of snootiness about him.

In the end, I spoke with the vendor myself and offered to help by speaking on her behalf to the BS. Now sometimes it pays to pull the *look at the publicity card*. I asked the staff at the BS what it would look like to the general public if they were to repossess the property from a woman with four kids whose house had burnt down and she had a broken leg. She asked, "How would they know?" I replied that I had the Sun newspaper on standby for the exclusive story if they were to go ahead with possession. You will never guess what happened next. Yes, you guessed right, they backed down and said they would put all possession proceedings on hold. Not only that, I got them to agree a sale to myself at £70k and that they would not chase the debt with the vendor. So as you can see, never rely on what the so-called professionals say. I did fall out with the auctioneer and he retired a year later.

Eye-opening stuff; we sold that property at the next auction for £85k.

Rule No. 3: Ignore the price

This rule has made me many hundreds of thousands of pounds and it's something I think many investors find hard to do. I know that an asking price influences people's decisions as they see it as the true value. Well it's not, and please remember it's an asking or starting price; it's not where you start, it's where you end up that's important.

I remember a time when I was speaking to an agent and he mentioned a property that he was having a few problems with; the property had been kicked out on survey three times because of a structural crack. The vendor had it on the market for £210k. I was very interested by this as it had all the hallmarks of a deal. I went to view it and the cracking was slight and what I would have called 'non-progressive' as they say in the trade; in other words, it was not going anywhere.

The vendor was panicking and the agent said she would probably take a good offer. She had already accepted £175k and that buyer, if he could get a mortgage, would drop his offer to £145k.

I was about to shock him and his client; I wanted to pay £100-£105k. The agent fell off his chair and said, "Why don't you speak to the vendor?" and I said I would. This is very unusual and I was somewhat surprised. I took the vendor through a process of negotiation which I will share with you in another chapter and after a short while we agreed a price of £105k. Now the thing was there was another property in the same street with its own drive and garage on the side for £299k so when ours went to auction I believe this helped us get £183k in the room. This was a shock as I felt it would sell for £125-£140k.

Now if I had not ignored the price, I would have paid a lot more.

Another time I had tracked a property through my follow-up system, this came on the market at £139k. An end-terrace property and it had been knocking around for about six months and going under offer a few times. It was a repossession and they have certain protocols and must adhere to this because they have a duty to the defaulting borrower. The agent said that their sales had fallen through just because of bad luck. I offered £90k and said I would not go any further. The agent thought I was taking the piss but, as she found out, I wasn't. What surprised her was they asked for proof of funds and they normally don't ask for this unless they are considering it. Now I would have paid more for this house but because of the fact they had asked for proof, I stuck to my guns. One week later I had bought the house for £90k. That's £49k off the price! Then we sold that house for £110k.

If you ignore the price you will have access to potential deals that you would otherwise have missed, as long as you keep in mind ConTroL because this is more important than anything else at the early stage when searching for deals.

Rule No. 4: Never offer the price you want to pay – take 10% off

I have mentioned this rule many times so far, it's a reflex for me now, I don't even think about it.

This came from my training as an estate agent; they trained me to start high with our fees so the vendor feels they have won something. One day I thought 'Will this work the other way round?' so I decided to try it.

I went to see a young couple who were splitting up, they had been let down by a previous buyer and were very keen to get a deal done. The agent gave me some information and said they were looking for £85k; it was on for £95k. The negotiating process I take you through in this book is very powerful; also this rule forms part of the stages of that process.

They said they really wanted to achieve £85k. This business is all about understanding how people perceive what you tell them and I know it's all about how you frame your questions or what you want to say.

This is how I did it the very first time.

"I would love to buy your house from you although I can't go to the sort of price you are asking. But I wish you well and thank you for the opportunity." Now I knew the agent had bigged me up as the guy that could help them and solve their problems. They said, "Oh, we thought you were coming to buy our house and that you had the cash." I replied, "Yes, I am here to buy it but not at the price you wanted."

They both looked at each other and he said, "So what would you pay?" I had not refined this rule at that stage and this was the early part of my dealing career. I would have paid £85k so I replied, "It begins with a seven." This gave me lots of room for movement and their minds were working overtime. Then I shut up; this is a part of negotiating where I see many people, no matter what products and services they are buying, screw up. The first one who speaks about the price loses.

People don't like silence and they said they did not want to go below £76.5k. Bingo, just saved myself £8.5k on the very first go. As you can see, this is very effective.

I teach this at the public speaking events that I do around the country and I have had so much feedback on this rule. You don't even have to restrict it to property. My solicitor tried this on a car purchase recently and got more off the price. He was so excited by how easy it was.

I received an email from a guy who had bought the house next door to one of his investments. This guy had already bought 16 houses and was what I call experienced, the seller was aware of what he had paid for next door. This guy had paid £60k for the original house and said he was prepared to pay me £54k. He did exactly as advised and the seller said, "But you have paid £60k for next door and mine's in better condition." This guy shrugged his shoulders and said, "That's my price." The seller accepted and my guy said, "I would have paid £60k if I had to." He saved £6k on that purchase.

Rule No. 5: Never get emotional about the deal

Those with a nervous disposition might feel a little ill with what I'm about to admit to you. Back in 2006 I was doing extremely well and I thought I was invincible. My ego was firmly in charge and I thought I was the big cheese. I was driving a very expensive car with my personal number plate and things did not look like they could get any better for me.

Now I have learned a lot since those days, but can you imagine me turning up for an appointment with all the local investors, dealers and developers? I turned up thinking 'I'm top dog' and wanted to prove myself and impress the agent. My emotions were raging and I wanted to win so I bid strong to blow out the completion. Well I did win, so I thought. The property was also round the corner from my house so it was my territory. Thinking back to it, I cringe now on how pathetic it was – all that ego and bravado. I agreed to pay £220k. In the second chapter I revealed about having strict criteria; well I broke all the rules that day, I did not make any sense whatsoever.

I still remember vividly the conversation I had with my partner about it. He said, "That's sounds dear, you sure we want to buy this?" I said, "Yes it's cheap and I know this area really well, this will sell for £250k all day long."

We placed it in auction and it never even had a bid; my emotions were about to cost me more than my battered ego. It doesn't matter how much you want to sell something, if no one is there in the auction to buy then it won't sell.

So off to the next auction. I think it had got round the trade that the great Paul Ribbons had bought a pup, because Richard and I had strong words about this and he said, "Let me deal with this, you are not thinking straight, you are too emotionally involved for some reason." He could see what had gone on and my cock-up was going to cost us big and I knew it. I felt sick, not because I was going to lose money, in fact I was sick because I was costing Richard half as well; I was responsible for that.

At the next auction Richard set the guide at £180k+ which I objected to and it sold at that figure. All told we held this property for close to nine months and the total loss was £56k. What a lesson, one I will never forget. My ego is very much in check nowadays.

Even when it comes to negotiating with people I know well, I now let Richard negotiate on my behalf – not because I don't trust myself, I just never want to be in that position again.

So be warned.

Another way my emotions can play a part is when we are low on stock; I have been known to buy things I would normally turn down. It's a trap I warn my delegates about: when you're desperate or frustrated you will sometimes make rash decisions. I have done this a few times in the past.

As you can see, these rules play an important role in the day-to-day running of my business.

CHAPTER 5

The people business

I often hear people say, 'I'm not in the property business, I'm in the people business.'

This is one of the most over-used clichés in the property industry. I must ask, though, do the people really understand what this cliché is all about? I don't think most investors get it. Most very successful people I know get it, but the average I'm not so sure about. And I will tell you why.

The average person is what I call 'stuck in I-mode' – they primarily put themselves first and are looking for 'what's in it for me?' and I think a lot of people find it very hard because we are hardwired to think of ourselves first. It's a survival instinct. I tend to get my clues of human behaviour from Mother Nature; she shows me clearly how life is so simple but we humans complicate it with our bizarre traits and rituals. We have a conflict between nature's code of conduct and society's code of conduct. Nature's code is 'procreate and survive at any cost, everyone is a threat so beware'; while society says we must get married, have kids and live together, treat everyone equal and love our neighbour. Now we have come a long way in our civilised world and I'm not suggesting people are having a big conflict with this, but if you understand that there is a small conflict, then it's easier to deal with people's odd behaviour, especially with people who could become a threat or stop us from getting what we want, like estate agents.

This is also affecting the sellers and agents – again they could be stuck in I-mode, there is a slightly different fear, which is more about being taken advantage of, and this is understandable.

I'm never arrogant enough to think that anyone else should have any consideration about my situation. I know they will not care a hoot and this does not worry me because I understand it's my job to get an understanding. With all the coaching that I carry out, I find the hardest thing to do is let go of the fact that if you see it from the other party's view it will not be returned.

So how does this subject affect my business? Whether its sellers, agents and ourselves, we are all people. The estate agent is a person also! Honest!

I want to ask you a question, "What do you think of estate agents?" No, don't laugh, I really mean it.

Most investors may have a few agents they get on with but generally they don't have a good word to say about them. I am aware that they can be very annoying but they do act for the vendor and not you. This is where most of our conflicts come from with agents.

I heard a saying recently; now I like hijacking someone else's sayings and if I knew who said it I would quote them, but I'm afraid I don't. But it did make so much sense to me because when I look at my business life I can see how this has affected my success. *'Your net worth is equal to your network.'*

When I first heard that I thought, 'What a load of crap,' but then as I was writing the first chapter it started to make sense.

Investors are sometimes amazed that when I'm full-on in my trading business I speak to at least 50 agents a week, sometimes up to 200 if I'm pushing things. I have a good rapport with hundreds of agents but rarely do I get offered deals from all of them; only a small percentage contact me religiously. And that's all you need to make a living. But I don't want a living, I want a lifestyle and that takes effort and a great understanding of how people react to things. I want to know as many agents as possible to increase my chances of success.

Listening skills

I have mentioned so far that very few people can see things from someone else's point of view because *they are stuck in I-mode*. I coined this saying, so I will take the credit, please.

Many people I meet are looking to see what they can get out of their dealings; they say they are looking for a win/win situation but never see it from the other person first. I know it may seem that I do the same with the case studies I share but, as I share with you in the Negotiating chapter, I want to find out what the situation is so I can understand the agent's and the vendor's predicament.

I often ask if anyone has read Stephen Covey's The 7 *Habits of Highly Effective People*. Many have, and when I press them on what the fifth habit is about, not one person can recite it.

'Seek first to understand then to be understood.'

It's interesting that he explains about the skills of listening.

I spent time in the Samaritans as a volunteer a few years ago and the training was a real eye-opener. They teach you to listen and not to have sympathy but empathy, and that is what Stephen Covey is on about.

'The greatest gift you can give another human being is to show compassion whether you like them or not.' Paul Ribbons

Empathetic listening is a skill I urge everyone to learn as it will improve your general communication skills as well as business.

So how will this help us find and negotiate great deals?

The reason I asked how you see agents is because they are people and I always empathise with them.

I had a client who was looking for property in the Midlands. He had seen a house that needed everything done and was boarded up. I asked him to ring through and get some info and make an appointment. He called me back and said that the agent would not give him any info and she was very rude.

I decided to call this agent and see how rude she was and do you know what? She was rude. But I don't give up that easily, do I? You know me by now. This is how I handled it:

"Hi, you know that property everyone and his dog are calling about?"

"Yes."

"Could you give me some information about like how bad it is inside and has it any structural issues and what are the circumstances of the vendor?"

"No I can't, I have not been inside so I can't comment, you have to have a look yourself," (in a very rude tone).

 Now I use the magic powers of paying compliments, understanding and empathy.

"Do you know how refreshing it is to talk to an honest estate agent? Most agents would have just told me anything just to get me off the phone."

"Yes, I'm always honest, I don't like to wind up buyers."

"Yeah, it must be hard, all these buyers chasing one house and only one can buy it, then the rest will have the hump and you get all the flack" (understanding).

"Yes, it's so true, anyway how I can help you?" (feels someone understands her and gives me what I want).

And she was very helpful indeed.

She told me that her colleague had said that it was structurally sound but please don't quote her and that the vendor was the local authority and that the kids had tried to burn it down as it was not a very good area. When I phoned my client he said, "You must have got a different girl." After confirming I hadn't, we compared notes.

This was not hard to do and it can be learned. Sometimes I still catch myself in I-mode. But it takes practice; start with those close to you, start to think what's in it for them and how you can help them get what they want.

In Covey's book he talks about listening with the intention of understanding as opposed to replying. Now I found this one of the hardest things to crack as we automatically listen with the intent to reply.

When you're having a disagreement and someone else is speaking, do you really listen to what they are saying, or are you preparing your reply so you can get your point across? Please think about this carefully.

In a conversation with a large firm of builders I had to put this to the test and trust it was going to work (that was the hard part, I was fearing loss).

I had reserved four properties off-plan and negotiated a massive discount. I intended to flip them and already had a cash investor who was going to pay me £50k profit as a fee.

Three months into the deal I had no contracts and their office rang to advise me they were pulling out of the deal as they had got their figures wrong. I believed they realised they could get substantially more and under-estimated demand.

Can you imagine what that must have felt like? £50k was going to walk away because someone had got their figures wrong and I had an agreement with a big company who should not welsh on the deal? I was very annoyed, to say the least. I felt myself getting emotional and started to talk like an idiot in I-mode; I was ranting and when I rant I talk bollocks. They said I could meet the sales director if I wanted. So I agreed to this and I told them, "I will bring my lawyer," so they were expecting a fight.

An appointment was booked for a week later. At the time I was studying for my coaching course and I was reading The 7 *Habits,* and guess what chapter I was reading? Yeah, you guessed it, Habit 5. This made me take stock and I prepared myself for this meeting in a different way. I was still apprehensive that it might not work as well as a rant to get my point across.

The day of the meeting arrived and I was early, as I normally am. They greeted me and asked where my lawyer was. I explained I felt no need to bring him.

The sales guy had come a long way just to see me; no other investors had requested this.

As I had taken up the opportunity, he asked me, "Do you want to explain your side first?" I said, "No, why you don't explain your predicament so I can understand more?" Now he was not expecting this, he had been told of this guy who was really pissed off and was bringing his lawyer and was going to be a real problem.

I listened to him explain the circumstances and

how they couldn't sell at this price any more, all the investors who had negotiated a discount were affected; it was not personal to me.

He went on for about 20 minutes and I nodded and when he finished I said, "So can I recap?"

And then I related his predicament back to him in very basic terms, using his language (the terminology he used, not my own). He was so relieved I understood his position and his whole demeanour changed. I then went on to say how difficult it must be for him and his staff having to cope with decisions others had taken and the messengers felt like they were being shot. He was completely different after that.

Then I hit them with it; I told him the absolute truth.

I was there to make a profit and I speculated on this type of thing, I said that I had my buyers lined up to take them off my hands at a big profit. So as he could see, I was losing out as well. But the funny thing was he was sympathetic towards my situation and I was making money out of his company – something they don't normally like.

I suggested there must be some middle ground and I put in a proposal to meet me halfway. I left it with him and within the hour I had an answer. He agreed to sell to me at the halfway point and I found out afterwards that no one else got any discounts whatsoever and he was really impressed with my manner.

This works every time. Never fails: *Seek first to understand then be understood.*

According to Tony Robbins, all human beings' needs come down to six things and in order to meet them they use a variety of different vehicles.

He calls them *Human Needs Psychology* and the six Human Needs are Certainty, Uncertainty, Significance, Love and Connection, Growth and Contribution.

Whilst all these needs are important in understanding human behaviour, I'm only going to concentrate on two as I have found that these are the ones I have most success with:

- Certainty

- Significance

Certainty

We all need certainty, it's a basic survival instinct. Think about what you need to be certain about.

We need to know we can pay our mortgage or bills, that we are able to buy food to eat and that we will be safe.

This business is fraught with uncertainty. It reminds me of when my ex-wife and I were selling her property in the early 90s; we found a buyer quickly and things were proceeding well. The survey was done for the buyer and everything seemed hunky-dory. The survey came back and the property's structure was questionable; there was a hairline crack under one of the windows. This was probably caused when the windows were changed a couple of years earlier.

Now this did not bother me, although remember I was an estate agent at the time. But my ex-wife was really upset. I said, "Don't worry about it, I'm sure we can sort this out." She was very distraught. This got me to asking myself the question, 'What's causing her distress? Is it the house because someone is questioning its condition?' We were both very proud of our home and kept it in tip-top order.

Or was it something else? Then it hit me she was now uncertain if we would be moving and all her mental plans were in question and it was then I coined this saying:

'It's the uncertainty of not knowing what the eventual outcome will be that drives people mad.'

Selling a property is supposed to be one of the most stressful things the average person does in their lifetime, and it's because of the lack of certainty.

We as investors need to educate ourselves to be able to understand these situations. We then can put forward a solution because this is what this business is about: solving people's problems. We can only do this if we understand the person who is in front of us.

Starting with human needs psychology, I can get a greater in-depth understanding of why people do the things they do.

Significance

This is the need to feel valued as a person; everyone needs to feel important and some people go to extraordinary lengths to get significance. If we think about estate agents, lots of them are looking for significance in what they do and when they are questioned, this questions their importance.

I see many investors who try and let the agents know they are well-informed and, without meaning to, they undermine the agent. They don't see how their actions can have a detrimental outcome.

This reminds me of a saying I read by an author called Stuart Wilde; he talks about getting underneath someone. What he means is to make the other person feel more important than you. I do this all the time. I don't care if it looks like I don't know what I'm talking about, as long as the agent feels superior to me for a short while as they get their confidence so they know I'm not posing any threat to them. Then and only then will they know what I'm about.

The importance of language patterns is also very important in the art of communication. But be careful as your language can have a detrimental as well as a powerful effect on people.

I was on a viewing once with a client and they were asking questions of the agent. They said, "I think this property is too expensive compared with the other ones locally."

Now there does not seem to be anything wrong with this statement until we think about it.

This will probably get the agent thinking, 'Who are you and are you an estate agent?' This was his reply:

"Well, we sell lots of houses in this area and I can assure you we would not put it on if we did not think it was worth it."

He is trying to justify price with a direct confrontation.

Now a better way to deal with this is how I do it.

Instead of questioning the price in that way I would say:

"Do you mind if ask a question? I was wondering, there is a house around the corner on for a lot less than this one; now I'm not an estate agent but is that normal? Or am I being a bit thick?"

This will not offend the agent as I'm not actually saying I think this house is too dear, but when you question a difference, he will feel the need to justify the discrepancy as he did in the first one. I would then ask:

"Is this property on for your price or the vendor's price?"

This gives them a get-out clause and you will then learn if he has valued at that level or if he has an unrealistic vendor. This usually reveals whether the agent feels the vendor is to blame.

Can you see how this is completely different from the first one but it's asking the same in a roundabout way.

Questions and the way I frame them are very important tools I use to get information from people and I have made it a habit.

Greed and fear

Another thing I have read a lot about over the last ten years is the driving forces of greed and fear.

After the stock market crash of 2008, Warren Buffett was interviewed and said, "I get fearful when people are greedy." He was referring to the greedy boom of the previous years when people's greed pushed up prices of the stock market and property. Everyone jumped on the bandwagon and without any consideration of if there could be a bust.

Then he said, "I get greedy when people get fearful." He knows when there is uncertainty in any market there will be people who are so scared they will sell at any price rather than have the pain of uncertainty.

This leads me nicely into ethics and integrity.

Many of my peers are shouting from the rooftops about having ethics in this business and I can see why they are doing so. Mind you, 'Thou protest too much' springs to mind and I believe it's because there is a certain amount of mistrust around our industry.

Let me make myself absolutely clear, I don't believe in ripping people off.

But we have to understand what our primitive drivers are. I do risk upsetting a few here but …

If you can imagine two lions in the Serengeti stalking a herd of wildebeest: there is a strong one – lean with very little fat on him and would be a lovely meal –

also there is a young calf being protected by its mother and, on the outskirts, there is a lame one which is weak and very vulnerable. Which one do you think the lions will go for?

The lame one – and why? Because they know that the strong one will be fast, the young one will be protected by the female and the lame one will be easier to catch.

Now I have done lots of research on this and none of the lions have been to hunting school. They don't even have mobile phones. They don't even have a strategy before they go and hunt, no obvious planning. Now I'm having a bit of a giggle here but the point is how the hell did they know the lame one would be the one to go for?

The answer is instinct. The funny thing is I take my clues from Mother Nature and I look for motivated sellers (lame situation). If I try to buy a property at a huge discount of 30% from an unmotivated vendor, what do you think they will say? The second part will be ---- off, I'm sure!

So it's the motivated seller who we are we looking for. And again we have to look at Mother Nature for our clues, because if the lions do catch their prey, they kill it quickly.

And my point? The execution has to be ethical. This is where you look for a solution. I will go into more details in the Negotiating chapter as to solutions and how I frame this. But you can dress it any way you like, these are the facts. Another way of seeing this is that the leverage is the same: a lame house that is causing a problem.

I use the term 'going for the jugular' and we know that's what our lions will be doing. So next time you are looking for deals, please understand that unless the world sorts out everyone's problems overnight and no one needs to sell a house quickly, you will be paying market value and then your purchase makes less sense.

CHAPTER 6
Negotiation

This chapter is about my favourite subject.

'It's OK to build rapport, we need this in everyday life; I would rather build a bond as it's so much stronger. The thing is you can only do this with trust. It's trust that creates the bond. Imagine having this with all your sellers.'
Paul Ribbons 2011

Here you will learn how to negotiate with a motivated seller and to get agents to come up with a figure that you want to offer without letting them know in advance what that figure is.

I love negotiating and I have refined my techniques using 25 years of experience and the many training courses I have been on, also from what I have learned from the negotiating masters out there. I have pulled learnings from people like Tony Robbins, Wayne Dyer, Stephen Covey, Peter Thomson and Richard Bandler.

Now it's not always been that way and I fell into the trap that a lot of the top property trainers and gurus fall into: believing that you have to build rapport with smarmy compliments and looking for things in the seller's home to get a common denominator. We all need rapport in our lives – in the supermarket, with our colleagues etc. But we are talking about the biggest financial transactions here and it's about time people woke up to the fact we need to have much more than rapport. Also, this won't work all of the time and only works when you have an understanding and speak their language – and that will happen accidently 30% of the time anyway.

This is like throwing darts at a board and I don't throw darts at a board. I want a much higher conversion rate than that and when you can build trust between seller and buyer this creates a bond. And a bond is so much deeper than rapport.

Because I have an NLP background and a good understanding of people, I have designed a seven-stage process to enable anyone to put these skills to good use.

How can I express this to you so you understand how powerful this process is? It was responsible for generating £299k profit on five private deals in 2006 – that's nearly £60k per unit.

So have I got your attention?

Let's get down to it.

How do you negotiate with real effectiveness?

Well, it's a process which starts with integrity and honesty.

Stage 1: Always let them know why you are there

I was listening to one of my mentors and he suggested to me that if I was to let the seller know why I was there before I was to start any negotiation or before any chit-chat had taken place, then I would take away any suspicion the seller had about what was in it for me.

He said that most negotiators inevitably tell the vendor the benefits of their service or product before they even lay any foundation. An example would be:

'Well Mrs Vendor, our company can do the deal quickly; this will help you with your circumstances so you can move on, blah de blah ...' The vendor is thinking 'Yeah that's great but what's in it for you, and it's going to cost me.'

You have to give the vendor what it is they want. In the People chapter you learned about people's needs. Sellers need certainty and that's what you are going to give them.

I had a call from a seller in south-east London who had a three-bed semi-detached property. This property had been on the market for about six months and the vendor had explained she had been messed about by a few buyers. After asking lots of questions, I found out the property had been underpinned 25 years ago and the insurance company did not want to reinsure; this was causing problems for mortgage buyers.

This is what I said within the first few minutes of arriving at the appointment. "Can I say before we go any further, we are property professionals and are looking at some stage to make a profit from this property; is this OK with you?"

The vendor was very understanding of this fact and thanked me for my honesty.

I have never had a bad response from this question, because now I have given the seller what it is they want: certainty, absolute certainty that I'm honest and this builds trust very quickly. And also when I come to state my benefits, they won't have any suspicion whatsoever because they know up front what's in it for me.

This is also the ultimate rapport-builder, a mutual understanding between seller and buyer.

Once this has been established you can move on to Stage Two.

Stage 2: Ask the seller to state their circumstances

This is to get the seller to confirm their position. In order for me to understand everything for negotiating I need to gain as much information as possible. If you remember, earlier we looked for ConTroL. I will be looking at this stage to reconfirm all I have got so far and, if necessary, find out more.

I asked her, "Can you confirm again what your circumstances are? I know we talked about the problems you have been having; I think I have a reasonable grasp but I would like to make sure I am up to speed."

Then keep quiet and listen

This is probably the hardest part of the process because, as you learned earlier, people need significance; speaking and letting others know they are intelligent helps people gain significance, especially when they can see they might be able to help someone.

You have to have faith that you will get your time to put across everything you want to. If you want to say something that seems very relevant but are afraid you may forget, write it down while the seller is talking; one word will be sufficient for you to remember.

If you interrupt at this stage you will more than likely blow it. All the stages are important but this one is the most crucial. I promise you if you get this right you will be amazed how this will transform your negotiating skills. This process changed my life; once I had used it, I started using it in all areas of my life.

I need to hear from the vendor in their language what the situation is. I want to have a clear understanding from their perspective and not my own. This is very important for the next stage.

I'm listening for their metaphors, stuff like 'It's been a weight upon our shoulders' or 'a millstone round our necks' – something of that nature. Then I can talk their language. I'm also listening for all the minor details that I can repeat back to them.

Now the average investor listens for the first minute or so then jumps in and informs the seller that they have helped people similar to them and this is what they can do; it is far too early for that.

This is what the vendor said: "I have had three buyers who have been messing me about and none of them can get mortgages so it looks like I'm stuffed. I just want to get rid of this place so I can move on with my life."

Now if we look at what she has said, she speaks of buyers messing her about, she is stuffed and she wants to move on. This is great info that I will use in the next stage.

Because the next stage is:

Stage 3: Reaffirm all that I have heard back to them

Again, you have already learned that the vendor wants certainty and needs to trust us.

I have mentioned before that the author Stephen Covey has influenced me and it's here I use probably one of the most powerful communication tools I know today. In the previous chapter I explained about Habit 5 in his book *The 7 Habits of Highly Effective People*. Now this habit 'Seek first to understand, and then be understood' comes in very useful at this stage of negotiation.

The trick here is to use the info you have just received and reaffirm back in their own words and metaphors. This is very powerful and keeps the rapport-building going because the vendor will have felt that they are understood. In the case of our seller I said to her, "It sounds to me that you have had enough and you mentioned you felt that you were stuffed. I can see that it must feel that way with all the problems you have had and buyers messing you about."

This is very effective as I have used her words to describe the situation. She replied, "At last someone understands."

If you think about your own experience with people generally you will come across people who are very much like you and you may have similar interests. The interesting thing is you may even state this in a metaphor. I hear this regularly, 'They speak my language.'

I know that lots of positive-thinking books and books on how to influence are based on rapport but, as I said earlier, I think this process goes a lot deeper than that. This process builds a bond between seller and buyer and that bond is built on trust. This goes a long way, because even if you don't do the deal now you stand a much higher chance of getting another go later.

When I learn something I always try and make sense of it, and when I learned this it made perfect sense to me.

Stage 4: State my position

I have to state here that now I always give the seller flexibility.

I lost a deal once; I was talking to a seller and said I could do the deal tomorrow and complete in days. She said, "I will call you tomorrow to let you know." She rang the next day to confirm she had accepted another bid because he said she could stay there longer than a few days. Because I never said I could give her more time, she went with someone else and I was gutted. I have never made that mistake again, I can assure you.

So I state my position clearly and precisely.

I said to our seller, "We are a property company who specialise in this type of property. As I have seen the property myself, no further investigations are necessary, no survey and the price, if we agree, will be the price you will get.

"I have cash available to exchange and complete ASAP. If you want the money straight away then that's fine, you say, "Jump," I say, "How high? You are in control. If we agree a deal I will make sure our solicitors do exactly what we agree.

"If there is anything you need then you let me know and I will deal with it, I give you peace of mind."

This sets up the next stage.

Stage 5: Give an alternative

Now most investors are so worried about losing a deal this seems hard to do. Why would you want to give someone an alternative? Let's think about this for a second: we have built trust with this seller from the moment we set foot on the premises so I want to build upon this trust and the bond I have developed. Also I am very sincere in my dealings with people and I think this comes across in my approach. I'm also very confident that if there is a deal to be done, I will be doing it and this belief helps a great deal in this process.

This is what I said to the seller in south-east London.

"Why don't you consider auction? This is a route we may have to take at some stage ourselves; this type of property normally goes well in auction. I'm not sure how much you will get, it could be a lot more than we would pay as this sometimes happens in auctions; it's worth thinking about. Also I have the number of a person who will definitely pay more than I would; I can't guarantee he will go through with the deal, but it's worth considering."

Again this is trying to help the seller and builds trust.

Because she had seen that I could give her certainty, that alternative was too risky for her.

The other thing about this alternative suggestion is, while I mention it, I say they will pay more than I will and this is part of framing which leads nicely to our next stage.

Stage 6: Frame the potential offer

You have to frame the offer in a way that seems bad in a way that is expectant of getting them to choke. I will always do this because then they expect the worst and also everyone's ideas are different. I will say, "We would love to buy your property; it meets all our requirements, but the thing is we are so far away on the price it's an insult."

Now you will get one of two possible answers.

Answer 1: "Thank you, but I will not give it away." I know now I will not be buying this property that day so I will thank the seller and leave.

Answer 2: "What's an insult?" If I get this answer I know I'm not far away and there is a good chance I will be agreeing something and I go straight into Stage 7.

When I spoke with the seller I said, "As I mentioned earlier, we specialise in this type of property. My concerns are that if we buy it and the costs are more than we expect, I might have to keep it long-term, and because it's not mortgageable we won't be able to get our money out and that restricts us in trading. Because of this I think I will leave it, as if I were to offer it would be insulting you and we are getting on well. I don't want to stuff you any more than you feel you have been."

Now I was not that bothered if she said no but her response is typical. She said, "Go on then, let me know what an insult is, I'm big enough to handle it."

This was a great response and what I wanted; now I can go straight to the next stage.

Stage 7: State your offer and then keep quiet

I replied, "£200k," and she said, "I knew it would be that, can I speak to my family?"

I knew I had the deal in the bag at that stage.

I did not have to keep quiet on this occasion but I do get resistance sometimes and that is where a lot of investors choke; they go on and on because they are not confident.

I hear this often: the first one to talk loses. The problem for most investors is that they feel they have to justify the price they have just offered. If you have done the job properly, then you won't need to justify the price you offer. Also not many people like silence when negotiating so they find themselves talking with what I call 'gap filling' or talking gibberish.

I always wait for the seller to say something before I do unless it has nothing to do with the price I have just offered. If I do get a stalemate I will ask them to think about it and make my excuses. I will call them later to let the dust settle as this process may shock some people, even though you have warned them.

The most common answers I get to my offers are: 'Will you go a bit more' or 'I was looking for a bit more.' Sometimes I get 'How quickly could you do it?' With any of these, you know you are close and if you have followed the Paul's Rules you have at least 10% flexibility if needed.

So is this useful? Try it the next time you have a motivated seller and practise it regularly. Remember when you first drove a car you were not as proficient as you are today (assuming you do drive). You can know something intellectually but not experientially, so practise this as much as you can.

The property in south-east London sold at £263k in auction and we paid £200k. I put this down to bonding – it can seriously increase your wealth.

A lot of investors dread negotiating with estate agents but if done well it gets great results. This is not as effective as the previous process but it works. It does rely on the agent's ability to put the offer forward; it will, however, help with them taking it seriously.

This is a completely different ball game.

So how can you get an agent to put in an offer that's substantially below its asking price without being laughed out of their office?

Most of the investors I know have major problems and avoid agents at all costs because of this one thing alone. They complain of agents not taking them seriously and, as an ex-agent, I can see why.

I also have problems with agents, but as I said in an earlier chapter, I see the agent as the solution and not the problem. This attitude has got me many hundreds of deals that otherwise I would have missed out on.

As with the seller-direct process, the same things apply here and that's why we have to understand what the agents want. I know from experience that the agent is targeted on certain things: viewings, instructions (new housing stock), mortgage appointments, solicitor's recommendations, offers, reductions and sales.

Sometimes we have to frame things in different ways and we have to here. I do this by getting the agent to accept things he would not normally do and it takes practice to do this skilfully. I have seen lots of my delegates do this and they have had real fun and can't believe it works so well. The trick is getting the agent to come up with the figure you want to offer. If you just offer a low price, what do you think the agent will do? Yes – think you're wasting their time.

So here goes.

When looking for properties that require work, I'm going to give you a scenario that replicates these situations.

The property needs substantial work and is on the market at a price that is not far off the done-up price so I have an uphill struggle. Let's say £110k.

The first thing I want to do is to get a baseline set, so in order to do that we need to agree a figure that the property is worth in great condition. Now this price will be different from the agent's price because not many agents value realistically. So my conversation will go something like this:

PR: "What do you think this property is worth done-up in great condition?"

Now the figure he comes up with I need to bring down because, as you will see, this has a bearing on the outcome of the offer.

EA: "£140k."

PR: "Is that realistic?"

EA: "Yah, all day long."

PR: "What if I was to ask you to stake your reputation on it and if you got it wrong I would shoot you?" That normally changes the figure.

EA: "£125k, I know I could guarantee selling it."

PR: "Now, have you got a calculator?"

EA: "Yes."

PR: "Great, can you put in the following figures?"

PR: "First £125k." (This property needs everything doing to it.)

PR: "Now can you take away the following amounts?"

- 125,000

- -3500 for heating

- -3500 for rewiring

- -5000 for d/glazing

- -5000 for general building work

- -2500 kitchen

- -1500 bathroom

- -3000 redecoration

- -1000 timber + damp

PR: "Don't forget we need to take off your fees, you will want a decent fee won't you?"

EA: "Yes of course."

PR: "Shall we say …"

- 3000 inc VAT

- 1500 legal costs

- 500 for unforeseen stuff like insurance and all that jazz

PR: "Now I like to make a profit, what would you expect us to make?"

EA: "£10-£15k."

PR: "So if we agreed at £15k how much is that down to?"

EA: "£80k."

PR: "You're joking. I can't offer that, can I?"

Now that price is the figure the agent came up with, not me, so he won't be saying, "Don't be silly," will he? He owns that figure.

Now imagine doing it the old way:

"You have that property on for £110k and I think it's too much money and I want to offer £80k."

What do you think the agent will say? "Jog on," I would suspect.

As you can see, two totally different ways of doing things with differing results.

CHAPTER7

Tips for success in property and mistakes to avoid

I think that if I had to sum up my success it would come down to a collection of things and my ability to learn from my experiences. I'm not afraid to fail or make a fool of myself.

I was watching clips of Will Smith and he was talking about work ethic and I could not connect with this. I don't like to think I work because work sounds to me like something that's hard, and I don't do hard. As I have mentioned before, I'm ruthlessly efficient, I will find the easiest and fastest way to do anything. One thing I always do is find someone who knows what they are doing and copy them quickly. Now I know copying can seem childish; as we got told as kids not to copy other people, it has a negative connotation. When I was about to press the pause button on Will Smith (God forbid, not something I would normally do!), the next thing he said about working was very interesting. He called it your ability to hustle. Now he had got my attention!

I can relate to it because I don't see myself working, I see myself hustling. This is what I do and what you read today is a collection of my life of hustling. Now I'm not talking about hustling on the deals but in the way I go about getting things done. I push hard and never take no for an answer, and this is what I believe Will Smith meant – and by the way, I always get what I want.

This is interesting; as I write, I'm thinking to myself 'Will my readers understand what hustle means?'

Hustle: verb (used without object) 1. to proceed or work rapidly or energetically: to hustle about putting a house in order. 2. to push or force one's way; jostle or shove ...

Well, to me it's fun and not hard; it's bartering and getting amongst it, it's learning the rules of the jungle, it's playing swapsies in the playground and understanding what life is all about. And it's what makes me tick. The essence of me is to hustle my way through life in the easiest way I can, enjoying every minute of every day. I'm in my element when I'm in the state of hustle.

So this leads me on to how I can help you with a collection of short cut hustles to find deals on the open market. So I have compiled a list of do's and don'ts. Now as you know, I already have Paul's Rules so these are a bolt-on.

I call these the Four Pillars of Success.

1. *Determination: – noun 1. the act of coming to a decision or of fixing or settling a purpose. 2. ascertainment, as after observation or investigation: determination of a ship's ...*

I think this goes without saying, you need lots of determination. I'm blessed to have big buckets full and it keeps driving me forward. I apparently get this from my mother who, by all accounts, had plenty; she must have done because she had three kids before the age of 20.

I remember when I wanted to get into the property training business I made a decision to do whatever it took to get what I wanted. I went all over the country speaking with Simon Zutshi doing whatever

I needed to do to get exposure. I wrote articles in magazines and nothing was too much trouble. I was so determined to succeed it was not even on my mind that I might crash and burn. Writing this book took a lot of determination when you realise I have done it in just under two weeks and I have dyslexia; thank God for spell checkers and predictive typing. Those who are close to me are so impressed because they know how much I have struggled in the past with reading and writing.

2. *Commitment: – noun 1. the act of committing. 2. the state of being committed . 3. the act of committing, pledging, or engaging oneself. EXPAND 4. a pledge or promise; obligation ...*

This also goes without saying really, but let me explain it like this. Imagine you knew a married man, he was loving with his family and he held a good job. They were very happy, he was always there for his family, he rarely went out and came home on time. Everything was hunky-dory. Would you say he was committed? Then you found out he was having an affair with his assistant at work but only during his lunch hour. How committed is he now?

Commitment needs 100%, not anything less because anything less will not mean as much. You need to be in a resourceful state to go the extra mile to really push through the tough times because they will show up. They did for me while writing this book. I got stuck when I found myself writing boring facts and that's not what I'm about. I'm so committed I looked for a way to push through this and then I remembered my firewalk with the great Tony Robbins. I did this in 2009 – Unleash the Power Within, Chicago USA. He teaches that before you walk on hot coals you have to put yourself in a resourceful state, he conditions his delegates. For me to push through that barrier I went back in my mind to 2009 and put myself in that exact state. Immediately I was back on track and it's the commitment that drove me to do this.

3. *Tenacity*

I remember in 1992 the property market was on its knees. The UK had just been ejected out of the European exchange rate mechanism (ERM) and this caused interest rates to climb to 15.5%. Now I know this sounds mad, can you imagine what that was like – 15.5%! Anyway I was working as an agent at the time and trying to sell houses, and I mean trying; it was not easy because of the cost of borrowing. We had repossessions coming out of our ears. I was dealing with one particular property on behalf of a building society (BS). I received an offer for this house and advised my client to take it. They said no. The buyer was very keen but his offer was some way off. I knew this was likely to be the best we could get under the circumstances and I made it my mission to sort this out. I phoned the client over 70 times over a period of one week. The thing is they complained to my area manager. He was not best pleased because he felt it could lead to the company not instructing us on any repossessions. Now I can understand his concern. He looked into the situation and realised that I was persisting because the market was falling and falling quickly and if the BS missed this opportunity they could well have to take substantially less. After sorting it out and the offer was accepted he brought me into his office for a bollocking. He said:

AM: "You are so tenacious it's ridiculous, do you know you could have lost the client?"

PR: "What's tenacious?"

AM: "It's when someone does not let go, it's like a dog with a bone."

PR: "Oh, that's good then."

AM: "No it's not; well, I suppose it has its uses."

When I got home I opened my dictionary to find out the exact meaning of tenacious and then I took his words as a compliment. I liked being tenacious.

Tenacious – *adjective 1. holding fast; characterised by keeping a firm hold (often followed by of): a tenacious grip on my arm; tenacious of old habits. 2. highly retentive*

This will help you when you find something you want, like a deal. I mentioned the importance of follow-up and this is where it will come in handy because I keep a firm hold on all the properties with agents that are SSTC and this has earned me £1000s.

And I thank John Spicer for pointing this out to me because I'm proud of it.

4. *Resilience: – noun 1. the power or ability to return to the original form, position, etc., after being bent, compressed, or stretched; elasticity. 2. ability to recover*

readily ...

Wikipedia: "Resilience" in psychology is the positive capacity of people to cope with stress and adversity. This coping may result in the individual "bouncing back" to a previous ...

This business is fraught with disappointments and frustration just as it is in life. But it's your ability to overcome any situation that will determine your success.

I was attending the Bucks property meeting and I'm one of those people who does not like to be late. I have to be early, so just in case I got there at 2.00 pm. Hang on, Paul, the meeting starts at 6, I told you! So I thought I would put some words down for this book. What I did not know was I had my wife's laptop and it has a different word processing package. I had my work on a memory stick and opened my chapter. I proceeded to type and I was rocking. The stuff just came out and it was all good; I managed to write half a chapter, about 2500 words. When I went to save it I realised it wouldn't save as it was a different format. I lost all that work! Imagine what that must have been like! Did it bother me? Of course it did, it pissed me off for about 10 seconds. But then I knew I had to just get on with it. This is only a small thing compared to other things I have had to cope with.

Do you remember when I told you my business partner and I lost £56k on one deal? What I didn't say was over the next 18 months we lost over £100k because the market changed. I lost my confidence and I did not know what to do. I would not buy a house for about six months. Now in hindsight this was a good thing. But the market changed in our favour and I needed to snap out of it. Luckily Richard and I did a charity pushbike ride to Paris. This was to challenge me being asthmatic and this experience inspired me because it reminded me of how resilient I am. My nature is to get on with it despite the odds or the enormity of the task in front of me. So when I got home I found pictures of all the houses I had been involved in over a five-year period and pinned them on the back of the office door (I call this my deal board). This gave me a reference to my previous success. I also read and re-read lots of books. The thing about books is, do you really get them? I heard something that I had to look up and it is this.

Someone once said to Swami Chinmayananda, "I have gone through the Bhagavad Gita several times, but nothing has happened." To this Swamiji replied, "You have gone through the Bhagavad Gita, but has the Bhagavad Gita gone through you?"

Wikipedia

The Bhagavad Gītā (Sanskrit: Song of God), also more simply known as Gita, is a 700-verse Hindu scripture that is part of the ancient Hindu epic, the Mahabharata, but is frequently treated as a freestanding text, and in particular, as an Upanishad in its own right, one of the several books that comprise the more general Vedic tradition. Apart from being a very comprehensive compendium of the whole Vedic tradition, it is also considered among the most important texts in the history of literature and philosophy.[1] The teacher of the Bhagavad Gita is Lord

Krishna, who is revered by Hindus as a manifestation of God (Parabrahman) Himself,[1] and is referred to within as Bhagavan, the Divine One.[2]

This is very true of books; it's OK going through a book but has the book gone through you? Now that's a concept a lot of people who claim they read should welcome. And this illustrates my point.

I used the books to regain my confidence and with the help of my deal board got back on track. 2009 was one of our best years and I thank God that I'm blessed to have so much resilience.

Act quickly

Another thing I'm blessed with is a sense of urgency. I act on things immediately; without hesitating I just get on with it. I see an opportunity and take it, run with it and make it happen.

I was talking with one of my friends and he said he had purchased a lead from a deal-sourcing company and asked me my thoughts. The thing with a lot of these leads it's about qualification and most of them are crap. Now and again you get a good one that makes up for the rest and I spotted a possible opportunity and said if he wanted I would deal with it for him. He left it for 24 hours and went on with his business. I contacted the seller within ten minutes and arranged for an appointment within the hour. When I got there and after talking to him I knew I did not want it and the deal was marginal; it needed light refurbishment and, although I sensed he was near to being repossessed, his mortgage was sizable and made it hard for me to do a deal.

Never fear, I was talking to an investor a few days earlier who was driving me mad to do a deal on a light refurb and kept asking if there were any deals he could do that I did not want. I called him from the appointment and he came straight round. We agreed a deal with the seller and this investor paid my friend a fee (which he split with me).

Two things happened that day. Firstly, the seller respected my sense of urgency and that showed him I was serious; he had others that wanted to do a deal but their lack of speed caused hesitation with the seller accepting their bid

Secondly, it gave him confidence in my ability to do the deal; if I was this quick to respond to the appointment then I could get things done for him.

What I see regularly is investors either do not want to be seen as too keen or don't put emphasis on speed. More deals are lost this way than any other.

So again, these are the Four Pillars of Success:

1. Determination

2. Commitment

3. Tenacity

4. Resilience

However, there are some very big mistakes people make.

Seven big mistakes most investors make

1. Gather irrelevant info

This I find most frustrating. Do you remember the doctor's analogy? That's what this is all about.

You need relevant info, remember the most valuable commodity I know is information, but it has to be relevant, otherwise what's the point? I see more time wasted getting the wrong info. Luckily for me, I learned this at an early stage as it was knocked into me right at the beginning of my property career.

2. Chase the wrong type of properties

This is another old chestnut; if they have the right info then you won't be here, but the number of times I hear people telling me that they have found a deal that is amazing. I was at a networking meeting when I got approached by a guy who was very frustrated about a property he wanted to buy. He was explaining that it was too much money and he had offered the vendor what he thought it was worth. I asked if he had checked the vendor's circumstances. He said the vendor had been left the house in a will and lived in Switzerland. Now I didn't know much about the deal but as soon as he told me that I said, "You need to double-check why he is selling because, I would hazard a guess, he does not need the money. The reason is if he lives in Switzerland, there is a possibility he is very wealthy."

I advised the investor about this and he said, "Yes, that was his reply when he first offered," and told me the man was stupid and did not understand that the property was not worth any more than his offer. This investor clearly did not understand that if someone does not want to sell a house at a certain price then they won't unless they need the money or are sick of it. This guy never had ConTroL.

3.   Ignore SSTC properties

Ignore these and there is a big chance you won't be making money in property. More deals are done after a property has been under offer than before because after a survey is done if there are any faults they are revealed at this point. Once this happens the leverage can be applied.

If you think about it, properties come to the market and no one spots their faults because the average person (and this includes agents) don't know what to look out for. Here's the thing, once a survey is done and a fault comes up that's the vulnerable time. If it keeps coming up, eventually the vendor gives in and sells to a buyer who accepts its problems; you want to make sure that's you.

4.   Never follow up

I have a filing cabinet purely for this subject alone because, just as with the last mistake, if you don't track them you will lose them so you need to have a system to track things. This is for when the timing is not right but I feel a deal could be done in the future. Again, more deals are done this way than when a property first comes on. Deals are made and not many are obvious.

5. Influenced by the asking price

Interestingly this is one that again many investors fall down on; they automatically assume that the asking price is the value so they are influenced by it. Remember it is an asking price, not a valuation. It's where you start as opposed to where you end up, and where you end up is more important.

6. Undermine the agent

People do this without trying, they want to get across that they know what they are talking about so they are always butting in on someone, or they state what they think in order to get acceptance. The other thing they do is try and show their knowledge by stating to the agent something like, "I feel the price is too high." Then the agent thinks how far apart you and he are. They may not say it but I can assure you they will be thinking it. If you think the price is too high, don't tell the agent, just ask questions to reveal the real price.

7. Use only a few agents

This one amazes me when I question investors that are struggling to get deals and I ask them how many agents they contact typically in a week and I get, "Well I have two really great agents I have a good rapport with and they are looking out for some deals."

Pah, get a life! As I said, when I'm on form and hustling I'm speaking to up 200 agents a week. I know you have to be in it to win it. I understand that agents who build good rapport will be building rapport with all the buyers, not just you. I never rely on an agent to call me because I cannot wait for them to call me. If I did I would be skint. You have to be amongst it to stand some sort of a chance out there. Agents are reactive and not many are proactive and that's what you need to do: become proactive.

You now have the foundation for a positive promising property career if you follow this collection of steps, stages, rules, tips and mistakes to avoid; you will stand a far greater chance of success in property. I don't know all the answers but I know what has worked for me and, more importantly, what has not.

If you want to take this further or feel that you could do with some more of this really cool stuff, then please come along to our Flagship one-day event Reveal Your Property Riches.

Please visit www.revealyourpropertyriches.com

I look forward to working with you personally very soon, and to your future, cheers and good luck.

About the Author

Born in Plaistow, East London, Paul began a remarkable journey. He was educated at an inner London school, but having undiagnosed dyslexia, struggled at school and eventually left without completing any of the exams.

After leaving school he worked within the baking industry and always dreamt of a lifestyle he knew he could and one day would attain. When Paul reached the age of 23 he realised he had lived longer than his mother had. This realisation had a profound effect as he made a decision never to accept mediocrity and to live every day to the full. Having bought a property at this stage in his life Paul took a gamble that was to change the direction and has shaped his life beyond his dreams.

He managed to "hustle" his way into estate agency. Here he was in his element and flourished, working his way up to manager and eventually being considered for an area position. Paul's people skills came through and while working he met some of what he calls his inner circle of friends – the ones you can count on one hand. Little did he know one of those friends would become so influential to the point they are still doing partnership deals today.

With the pressures of divorce and the big dream of freedom, Paul became frustrated at the restrictions of working for other people and made the decision to go it alone. He left estate agency to pursue a career as an acquisition agent with a distinguished list of clients. Then on one fateful day the partnership that became the foundation of Paul's illustrious dealing career was formed. Together they have done many hundreds of transactions, making huge profits as well as some losses. Paul's philosophy still shines through; nothing is beyond any human being; you just have to want it bad enough and remember you're in the people business and never forget it.

Having a great understanding of people and their needs, Paul then met Simon Zutshi who encouraged Paul to share his knowledge. So Paul embarked on a speaking tour for Simon's Property Investors Network (PIN). Paul's no-nonsense style was well received and he became in great demand. In his seminars Paul now teaches hundreds of clients how to find profitable properties via the open market. The basis of his philosophy is still about understanding people.